T0302500

Sheer Indefinite

Selected Poems

1991-2011

Skip Fox

UNO PRESS

Printed in the United States of America

Skip Fox, 2012

Sheer Indefinite: Selected Poems, 1991-2011

ISBN: 978-1-60801-080-6

Library of Congress Control Number: 2011944341

A majority of the poetry herein appeared in *Kabul Under Siege* (Bloody Twin Press, 1991), *Wallet* (Bloody Twin Press, 1997), *Fighting Kiwis* (Oasis Press, 1999), *What Of* (Potes & Poets Press, 2002), *Adventures of Max and Maxine* (Auguste Press, 2003), *At That* (Ahadada, 2005), *For To* (BlazeVOX, 2008), and *Delta Blues* (Ahadada, 2009).

Book Design: Megan McHugh.

Cover photo: Skip Fox. Cover Design: Bill Lavender and Rikki Ducorret with the assistance of Jerry McGuire.

Illustration on page 47: Tammy Charron.

CONTEMPORARY POETRY

UNO PRESS
University of New Orleans Press
unopress.uno.edu

Contents

Sheer Indefinite

Selected Poems

1991-2011

There is not a phase of our experience that is meaningless, not a phrase of our communication that is meaningless. We do not make things meaningful, but in our making we work towards an awareness of meaning; poetry reveals itself to us as we obey the orders that appear in our work.

–Robert Duncan

from *Kabul Under Siege*

Angels

Rome, *March 14.*
At the recent Vatican Council on the Nature
and Existence of Angels, one cleric, an American,
suggested better use be made of the guardian variety,
that they be trained, say, to shag and eat mosquitoes
or cockroaches, transport pleasing scents, remove others,
filter cigar smokes (there are several), or control
the aura's temperature by a few degrees–nothing, of course,
which would interfere with their ordained duties: a sharp eye
for troubles and opportunities

that they can be blue, milk
lemon, cool red, with or
without wings (everybody
has one–Salman? Yazdi?)
that they are of the morning,
superseding mosquitoes

It is an angel drives my car
when I write

In the valley between her wings,
where the mind rests, is the source
of the abstract

The boy who threw himself from a cliff was propped
against a large rock by an angel who tied a bandanna
about his leg. She told him that she was a little boy, too,
but he knew that she was an angel. She kissed him and petted him
and with her small hand in his told him stories which he forgot,
but he knew how good they were because the pain was gone
while he listened.

The mind can become an angel of
perfect sorrow

ii Where They Live and What For

Every cat has an angel behind its brows
There are ruby-throated angels; a red angel
  hums across the turquoise floor
Angels want *the simple naked truth*
They live in the gloves of great boxers (Lupe
  Gutierrez and Jeff Franklin!), in
  the boxer shorts of great lovers (no
  names, please), in the voices of
  Roy Orbison and Renata Tebaldi (all art
  beyond itself), in cement kangaroos
  on the playground (they stalk the
  package liquor store at night), behind
  the ribs of the emperor penguin (its
  skeleton
angels are in the light that permeates the
  blinds, in the water that fills
  the toilet tank (there are also
  outhouse angels that sweat and burn),
there is an angel in charge of nocturnal
  emissions, and an angel that lives
  in the heart of Russian novelists (her head
  gets stuck in the tricuspid valve
they live just past the line of sight, riding
  waves of thought
it is angels prepare the synapse between
  lightning bolts

iii On the Causes and Cures for Angels

The angel is nothing the poet
said, our *more furious self*, projected
on the darkness, otherwise
everything we do or have, and comes
with its own cure: a tiny head
upon a stick, sewn mouth and eyes perhaps

The Garden of Earthly Delights

i

The rock rolls free.
Dragon smoke. Louisiana
shine. The mystery voice
drawls, 'Civil rights *for*
white folk.' My friend,
the Republican, takes a
let's wait and see. Others smile
that quiet . . .

  Miracles of the Virgin in Tickfaw, La.:
    'a spinning and bursting of the sun'
    (snapping insects of sight

Free! Who's been on death row,
beneath the sheet, tagged toe, now
released, *a new man*, on his own
recognizance. (How does he know
who is he?) *Eenie, meenie* . . .
What hell does he advance, *tiny*
head beneath his cloak

Enid Dee, coiffured (her wig), bruised
(body), missing lower teeth (being made),
a ripening 63 (65), said, 'Build me a small fire,'
to the crowd, 'What my Daddy told me' (to
herself)
      'Mother of God, our Mother, Mary
      most holy' (to no one in particular

ii

She turns on the tip
of his tongue. Everything
he says she is, a dance
of flame, wind shot,
a net of silver fish.
She cannot forgive
him this

But what is he, having
done? Who is left to bring
him to himself? And when
will he come to?

iii

In The Garden of Earthly Delights
a tree stands with fat, black *fruit*
of my life. An angel pecks its eyes.
Above ash heaps, *where once were men*–
knowledge divorced from action, actions
devoid of sense–sift the various windes,
the various minds, through which
a gargoyle laughter descends, the refuse
of another year.
                    A lone youth leaps
into the Vermilion River, mud brown,
and lands in the bloated corpse of a cow
in which he sticks. A small voice tells him
to raise his arms and slide through.
He does and drowns. And that's the truth.

iv

He wanders through the ruins of sleep
ground zero of snowfall,
garden of skins
He is softest man, animal
who would kill black Adam
and whitest Eve
an assassin exhumes bleeding schoolgirls
from memory, tracks them
through tainted snow
He steps over things, on things
in bodies, bodies becoming
things, counterweight

The Siamese angels, Angelo and Luigi, rise
above the horizon on which he lies,
as far as the eye can see, headless,
in the dawn
Joined at hip and wing-tip, toe to toe,
their single halo scrolls a loping figure eight
in the early shards of light
They dip their wings in tepid pools beneath
his collarbone, drip green and brown
across his belly's burial mounds
and light upon his sex, ringed
with black memories, to preen
until it chimes. He has arrived
at the *heart of the heart of delight*.
And they?
They've done their part, fly off to the jazz
of Bourbon Street, where he keeps the beat.

Year Zero *(prime time*

Outside
the first sounds still bounce
off trees in the dawn. Each
moment murders the last

He sips
sharp coffee, hot as the dew,
rose that opens the first time
each morning

Wakes to the smell
of steak and eggs, roadkill
and biscuits

Walks the same
garden as Adam, between
like alternatives, accompanied
by kindred spirits, bat
and butterfly, lizard
that pilots the jay, stones
that live so much more
surely than ourselves . . .

'Me at last' (great god

terror at the edge
of each leaf

The Garden of Earthly Delights II
Promised Land

i

O Enid, where art thou? Where hast
thou gotten to? Where are thy tiny pursed
lips? The tight curls pasted
against thy forehead? Where are the delicate creatures
of thy neck? Thy camisoles and stays hanging
behind the barn? O Enid, in thy young youth
did someone pull electric silk through all
thy tender circuits? Was the air forever brighter
before thy footstep? Thy porch washed
in the butter of song?

Enid, didst thou call out among nights
as dark slashed against thy bunk?
Did thy bones rise through bedclothes and flesh
to search the hollows of his palms? Did he forsake
you, Enid? Or did he avenge himself on you
your youth?
                    Enid?

ii

Let her fingers be ten as the ten hearts
    of the river, river within river, etc.
And her mind various as the winds but close
    that her counsel be not spread abroad early or
    too late
Let her voice be certain, indelible as the egret
    amid green shallows
And her tongue one that it might measure her

thought: the twelve constellations, colours
  of mud under a gas lamp
Let her skin be of the sun, as dark as the sun
  in mind's dark, a bruised berry, that
  her urge be sweet as street garbage, her sweat
  metallic on the tongue

Then breathe on her as on a bowl of waters, let
  her heart beat deep within, her seals expand
  against the ring of rivers, her gates swing
  shut against the several winds
And knock, call soft within, 'Above all others,
  perfect one, my dove,' spice dripping
  from the latch and from the fingers
Then steal on her, speak close as in a chamber, loosen
  all her limbs, and plant an alphabet within
  that the word grow hard upon her

'sister, my dove'

iii

Came they then to Tickfaw, to
a canefield outside Tickfaw, like
ants they came to see
the virgin in the noon
day sun
    roaring arcs of sunglobs
from her hands and feet,
and where her heart had been,
    'a spinning and bursting of the sun,'
and where the world . . .

a hole
  dark

as Akhenaten, black as black
shit, Nile mud and blood to
wall them in to wall
them out

then how shall I tell of my love?

her small feet on the altar steps, in time
with the wingbeat of bat and butterfly, fragrant
as honeysuckle, her dance, petals of foot
fall on smooth stone, her shadow leaps
from stair to stair
to stair
in strict proportion
to the priests' amaze, the laughter of angels who,
riding the Nazarene flowers of her hair, swoop
low to lend support to an errant toe curled over
an outer edge, or a heel adrift in cerulean space . . .

Χαιρέ! Χαιρέ!

while the dusts of kingdoms rise from her feet

then how shall I tell of my love?
and to whom?

Enid?

iv

The morning's ripe. Light
oozes from every pore

as out of the condemned
fresh from his dream.

If we could crack her open
like a bat, sweet wedged
fruit, we'd find
a swarm inside
fed by bees
                    Yet
she remaineth on his finger, in the ache
of his tongue, his chest, his eyes, her
flesh surrounds him, her look his
narrow bed. And yet
he'd do it all again and
yet again

                    Honey hath entered the honeyhead.

            he twists in his cell of sweet
light, the buzz of angels all around, reads
strange figures (bird tracks, the hearts
of small animals) on the wall, watches
the moon and sun pass backward before
him, makes intricate calculations
on his thumb, and waits, drunk
on the distillates of her blood–queen with whom
he'd mate, 70 ft. say, above the grasses
of paradise, to fall back
                                        complete,
having done with having done

v

This is the law of first things.

This is the law of oblivion.
Here, the quivering tit
above the void

                    (a hand reaches . . .

Here, the mosquito's hymn.
Here, the praise of bat and butterfly (they
    are Legion), giant fruit rising
    from a dog's grave, a tank rusting
    in the afternoon, azaleas
    on fire

This is the law.
We have seen it.
It holds forth from every crevice.
Surer than gravity, brighter than wine,
    lustier than our favorite general.

We saw it from Pisgah. We looked down
and there it was.
                    It eats
into our eyes, scalds our hearts,
steams our lungs, sinks and burns
in the coiled sump of our
intestines.

It is ours.

                After we have traveled so far.
After the diaspora of the self: the bull, the ball
of fire, the swan, the golden shower, the bestial
dove

        Χαιρέ!   Χαιρέ!

How tell of her? How?

She is everywhere, smiling flatly
from the wall of her indifference,
daydreaming from a thousand shades
of brown and green, a cheap yellow
behind her.

Χαιρέ!

You are mine (she whispers in the death cell)   A cramp
in the toe (to the climber)   I am with you, even
now (to the suicide)   She's asking for it (to
the rapist

Χαιρέ!

How tell?

that, at the break of noon, she hangs in midair a moment
before the plunge, he grabs her with hind legs, holds
her about the stomach, tears her skirt and short
shorts, her blouse and gown, she falls back, he holds
a knife at her throat, cuts her neatly beneath
the eye, it steams, his wings support them, they fall
through clouds, through mountain ranges, roll over
and over, he turns her, sticks it in, an often audible ejac
ulation, angels screaming, it catches, breaks off, steam
rising from the flowers from the lake

Χαιρέ!

The law. Like pheromones radiant from every pore

Don't you like it here
What's the matter (to the corpse

flatly she smiles	everywhere	brown and green	from the wall
the world stopped	birds still	in their flight	the word stuck
in cave mouth	light leaps	they are falling	over and over
she is dancing	on the steps	the dust rises	unto the law

falling through lakes, through reason, the hardness of cement, the
hour has come, now, falling

The Boat

From the sweat on the death cell wall at dawn
From the suicide's incontinence, the wet dream
    of the hydroceph: vinegar mixed with spittle,
    sweat, blood, and gall
From the serpent's mouth, the priest's chin, the eye-
    patch of the supplicant
From the oozings of the battlefield stuffed on the first
    wave (all between 13 and 8), sweetest land
    to crow's discerning tongue
From the basin of her vagina, choked with the seed
    of eighty-nine phyla, the gangbang of five-thousand-
    nine-hundred-and-ninety-five years
                                        etc.

                    come the drops   one

                                    by
                                            one

leeching through steel doors, the iron gates
    of the universe, the crisp pillowcase
    of the Vice President
through dream, the walls of comprehension, championship
    boxing, the footprint of an angel
through asphalt, recipes, Mexican suburbs,
    titanium and silk

                              a trickle

        streamlet to the lip at cliff edge, curls
        over, glistens across the streaked face, black
        and red, then falls into a mountain stream, a coil
        of pitch in hard blue, dark as ice, as munitions,

falling through centigrade, through memory, through
the riverbed, emerging on the other side, in a valley
of coughing mosses, the glimmer of lichen,
decay

            to caress the hull of our boat
that groans as we step in, push off
through weedy march, leaking . . .

                                        One ear
on the oarlock, one on the breeze, bitter
as a benediction, we stare into night's
socket, searching for the black scroll
of the opposite shore. Birds fall
through thick air; mosquitoes drip
into silence. We lean over the side, reach
a hand in . . . and draw a blank, a headache
without the pain. We pull it back, dry,
as though it had never been

Autobiographies

The story starts anywhere, useless

to describe, the sound of rain at night, not knowing
how long we've been awake, his boyhood
dream of gynecology, staring at the swamp
all day. (What to do on the weekend?)
How

the yard expands as though time had too much
frontage, the Teche backing up, salt
in its gut, and a well of dark beneath the leaves–they
are saying what they cannot. Maybe we'll really get it
this time. The wattage of a good resurrection could
set it off. Maybe the elevator stops and a truck
refuses to start.
Would a snuff flick scratch
that narrative fetish? Being in one, I mean. Or
or tracing your grandmother's line up some black hole
to Scituate or Rodmarton Halt? Here, the deepest itch
always happens to *the next guy*. Like the lottery.
Or lightning. (Who wouldn't want God's finger on
his poke?)
As if someone who has just died begins
telling a story to someone who's been here
all the time. I think that he was thinking that
I thought. . . [1] And the air goes white
with understanding. Fairy voices.
Or in the morning

barefoot, amid sun and lively shadows, a cool
breeze, he sets out and into the world, the gleaming
woods, to seek his fortune.

---

1 *Cred' io ch'ei credette ch'io credesse. . . .*

Reading a letter from

his mother, sunlight rushing the edges, shadows jerked
at his hand. Or directions (where to ford? what's in a mountain
pass?) from those who'd gone before, a map. From which
unfolds . . .
                                        Suicide always seemed beside
the point. Inexact. An increasingly inadequate
response.
                                                                                Around the next
bend, the sheer lake, colors tighten in the wind, voices
from the earth blow off, and the air that blurred arms and
chest moves at last like unmelodious whistling of indefinite
duration.
                                        Or driving for days just to reach the out
skirts (the ego hath such distensions), arriving at the clue
less present in time with a punchline dark as inner city (nowhere to
leave from, nowhere to go), cancellation burning our hands

                                                                                                                        as once

there was a man walked into a bar without a lisp or twelve-inch
pianist, never caught a leprechaun, etc.
                                                                                        or driving into a culvert
for a swift *vacuus ex machina*, meeting the wind on its own
terms
                        as it turns in the high trees above, fronting the whole land, abrupt
and insistent, as the wind in him turns into the jest, the last gas
station for a thousand miles and nothing beyond that lucent
mass moving into present

Meanwhile. A lull, like dying of yellow

fever after selling you brother's estate (in Texas). Lapse you
don't have to deserve. (Is it always hot and windy in lower
Missouri?)
                    Dearest! You're the one love of my life. There has never been
another. Not really.
                                    All day stood, a stare or busted thumb, nose
to rock face, as though both eyes opened on the glass and light
came streaming in, alive. What is that shadow burning at
his edge? Its dark flames fold back the plot, searing the marge
of what he isn't (by definition). Or is it silent as that whirlwind
across the plain?
                              In the moment before the explosion,[1] cloud balancing
on cloud, his exposure was precise, a man stepping over his own grave
on his way to the family reunion.
                                                            Dearest. The horizon is lost,
and I am caught on the gleam of surfaces, escape unfolding at the sides.

                                                  As though,
                              spinning off, he might collide
            with the self returning
from the peripheries of circumstance, a corpse
   fresh from the void crowded
      with event–an audience with the queen, advice
         from the corporate head (next time, you're
            dead), the sheared pin–nothing
                                                    to be
                                                      said, ex-
                                                            cept that coil
                                   of wind (a locomotive?) rain all night
                              the fever broke and seeped into our dreams (he spoke

---

[2] *having reed order fro the Governor to look to y*^{e} *powder & ammunition of y*^{t} *town, he went to y*^{e} *house of Goodman Tucker where y*^{e} *magazine of y*^{t} *Towne was, wch was but two barrels of powder & opened y*^{m} *& while y*^{e} *said lieftanant was drying some of y*^{e} *powder, abroad upon boards and doores, by some accident, G. knows what. . . .*

to fairies and those who lived in weeds), first
good sleep in weeks, until he woke to distances
not his own, a mountain range or layer of new snow, clouds
in their processions, as though there was a world to go to, get lost and love
in, and with only the future before him, find his own true, etc.

Dearest. Even
with others, I only thought of you. Please believe me.

Did the rocks thunder

within? Steam rising from the mouth. Too hot to burn. The sorrel colt
shaved to an ash.
What is it to be cast into a present beyond
extent-pulse shaking the horizon, treeline etched in dew. As though
in the predawn, you could crack open the outer dark where lucidities
contend and slip into a sequence in which nothing happens, the last
dream of the man who wrote, In the morning I will blow my brains out. What
then?
then
Will the glistening sides of the moment
collapse? Like a comedy, or coma? Midnight smeared his eyes. Even the back
glare before rain at night is of more consequence-light through which the lake
recedes.
And so he passed into the land, world of sheer exterior, rock pitch and edge, e-
late, or lying, soft, diaphanous, the babbling of shadows in deep shade, a silence, dark at
edge of pane or drop, that even the dead man's dream cannot penetrate.
Can there be edge
without extent? Luminous present between surfaces. Or is the world of less account than
the tales thereof?
He woke up and opened the door on nothing. Or rode west, across
the Great Divide. Drank his juice and coffee. How could it be? Even *there* wasn't there.
He saddled the shivering colt. It was impossible.
Yet there it is. Cliffs hang from
its opening light, boulders lurch from its sides, and at night, beneath its scattered
brilliancies, he shakes at its imperative. (Or could the Colonel and his men, caught
out, be saved by most delicate apperception?) The freedom of a man waking up
in flames, the seed of the house bursting inside him, mote that brings down
heavens, as though the door of his life stood wide open, the street clean, alive,
darkness glistening above the lake,
as a man, beyond antecedent, crosses
the threshold, *from nothing to start into being,* rising like the sun over the horizon
of event, and mounting the abyss between the entitative and operational aspects
of the soul . . .

I have never been alive before this moment! I have been dead until now.

Avalanche of lightening and opening of graves. Or cave-in, barge over-turning in great heat.

That willingness of heart facing the vast wilderness or 38

pharmacies with a shotgun. The frontier lay on him like the silence above a shallow grave (does it expand before the rain?) or all the street names of his hometown.

Nothing

in the visual field infers the eye so much as forward motion–as though emergent form rose each moment from the landscape to involve us again in the mystery of seeing.

Jumping into other people's lives as the arc of the *hora prima* sweeps across lawns and fields, fresh from the hood. Into those blue, elastic intervals in the distance (as over mountains).

He rode that spirit of knight errantry into the New World (I want to be a junkie!) as though he could escape the meagerness of plot–maybe he could make the rim before gravity began. (*Sweetest stand of timber. All the way to Mexico!*)

Climbing the bench

on the southern flank,   An excavation of light!   biomorph amid granite.   (Who lives in the depths? Beyond this universe of words stretched across low-relief space.) Or deliquium, into darkness's green edge, as at evening camp, searching the narrative beneath shadows.

What did you mean to see? That intervention, as a set of new themes–mobility, rearrangement, regulation, and interaction–of a "product" upon its "code" could play a fundamental, *constructive* role (reaching back to the Atlantic coast and even the Old World. Or *the structure of remembering what is not a dream.*

Where is light from in

this pocket, walking the folds of clouds. Absence of dark, backlit, or the dilation of all things. Luminescence at the base of trees, vibrance on the peripheries–as though sight were ignition and the world in flame. The surfaces expand and are consumed, their edge's radiance residuum.

Then how shall he enter his own life? As into enormities of rock and sky, carved by the sun, primordial mass staring into vacancy. Or naked, on hands and knees, teeth in the calf of his wife, as *up to the eye and soul* . . . where light pours over the horizon, sweet as heroin, sentient

until opening, interval as between a tree, what you thought, when the mind slides off and into . . . before we knew we were awake, thinking, with (as though there were objects there and not in here until you looked, while light, although unsteady, wavered through it seemed a screen or membrane, and the roof, crumbling, began, then broadened into fields, and voices with close insistence came, infinitely fine and isolated, no urgency, but as in weeds or music,

Ice that is not ice yet
no longer water. Indians
that are only rivers going
nowhere. Fog in which
no wagons gather

& into the New World on trails that could be tracks or insects, twigs, inscribed upon this land without history *(revealing the course of universal history?*

Native in native land . . .

Even the least story begins nowhere, in

the webbing of what is not, by definition, cannot be touched. He shot himself three times
in the heart. Etc. A busted flush. (In the city he was glass. A fluted reticence against
the dawn.

Wind blows through
the stars. Dream
and the beginnings of
dream. Urge, is it, or full
blown? Inklings squirm
on the horizon.

Yet how he *does* persist, as language does, emptied out, as the West
was (What? Crossed spears over space (where was light sown), the abyss be-
tween syllables, narratives, luminous field stretching out, the polluted body
of history, scattered, leaking, the set in the skull, a primal lust bounding
the perimeters (madness is indefinable), hunting all day, a mess of ragged
stars at night

Dream and the beginnings
of dream. As mountains, folded
into silence. And a river of voices
in the vacancy. Water petals over
rock face. Wind sharpened
on branch or twig. End-
less reticulations
of insects.

) All that is not / flowing
through all that is (

Came to these dark cliffs and streams, towering
abeyance of the present, where the one world never turning
from itself exists in glyph of ice and rock, magnetic spirit

design of dawn, and in the interior of event, its lustrous, sheer distances, as the distances in him, canyon and mountains, the anvil of the land, a thousand miles to get lost in, to lose himself . . .

or does not.

The petals peal, fold
back, in the stream un-
folding, wavering lens of light
on rock, spring in late
autumn, tidal pulse pulling
the melodic line through the
entire range, high plains to
ocean valley, all day,
all night

the relaxation and dilatation of the heart cavities during which the cavities are filled with blood.

Wallet

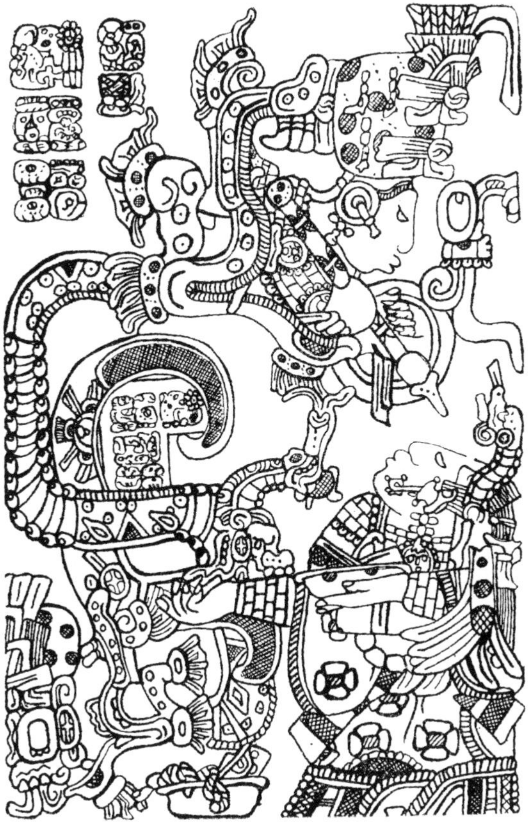

Even the least story begins nowhere, in the webbing of

what cannot be touched, by definition. Between the transmitter
and Spicer's radio. Deep space. "The primitive does not
exist" (Todorov). Before beyond. What's beneath
the word. The world we say. Names of the gods beneath
the week. Beneath numbers, what? "No narrative
is natural (beneath time), a discourse, not a series
of events." I hear with my words, not really
mine. How strange and true. As into a widening
gap, metaphor and the basis of metaphor, *a* and *ox*, "a sense
of proportion plugged into an unmeasurable," in-
cantation, faith or spell, "the transformation concepts
undergo before magical discourse is possible,"
the first concept before there was a concept.

Even the least story begins nowhere, in the webbing of

what is not, by definition, cannot be touched. Deeper or beyond
that, why not most near? between the inner
and neurotransmitter. Could we turn to it, then, attend
whenever (steep coma?) or do we, as deep
space? Would I have it angel and cross
to that effect? Why not. Or nothing, *na-*, with
out stretch, zero (the logician), granite leaning over
the abyss. Lost. Or walk where Adam walked, world of apple
and ox (magician?), heart of a moth. Letters blooming
in the sensorium, fresh from the husk. I would have
it angel gapping the plugs between *a* and
the, a compass, plucked string over synapse, S.O.S.,
all knees and dashes, tremolo buzzing the twat.

what cannot be touched, by definition. Between the transmitter

and the shadow leaning over the radio. Mayan? Listening as vaporous,
rusty, granite ear to gap. What cannot be thought cannot
be touched. Then everything is primitive, including
Todorov. What if the shepherd of being lived in that
ear? Attentive to the shadow, from which, It is the mind
creates the finite. The drift glistens. An ancient
civilization. Imagine a country boy in the city for
the first time. How not have the sense that the definitions
are more given? Two warriors in headdress. How not have
the sense of a shadow poised over a radio? Evening, almost
night. Does he look into those faces whose eyes exude
darkness? He finds his own pitch as jet, through moving
planes of color, as they loosen, dim, life in the interstices.

and Spicer's radio. Deep space. "The primitive does not

reveal the radical (though he may resemble it). How many
words does the Eskimo have for snow? Whence the cold
beneath the wind? *Ganik*, ghost within the storm, and *aput*,
ghost on the ground. (Or would it depend on the Eskimo?) And why
the desire for 17? They are as they are. And we as we. Believing
man might inhabit the land, not merely live on or off it. Dwell
therein. As in ear or mind. Attentive to the purely
possible. (How many do you have for *ghost?*) As though
you could tune into a tern as it oils its wings. Or a word that rises
from the root. The bodiless serpent climbs into the most desolate
regions of the sky. Flashes above the raw flesh eater on
his floe. It casts an eerie correspondence on the notion of what is–where
resemblance disappears into identity, spirit into new fallen snow.

exist (Todorov). Before beyond. What's beneath

the world? Rhyme and the absence of rhyme. Pulse keyed
to mind or heart. Prior to extent. The first awareness of what
we are the primitive. Man and woman in kayak. (Date
unknown.) Surrounded by presence. Having come into *the steadiness*
of its shining. Before being or in front of existence–that *state of*
permanent decision. Out there and here at the same time. Tighter
than a canoe. The future sings to its return. Esse. A jungle
of Eskimos. And between, climbing in between, the poem. Middle
of two. A man in the eye where the man in the eye would
have been. In an echo of light. (Who has not sensed the world
within? Granite. In carnate. Sheer moment and its companion. What?
Intelligence of the moment? That which does not vanish at
the end of resemblance. I am. The bearing across.

the word. The world we say. Names of the gods beneath

the what? Absence at the heart of every angle. Say your daughter gets
robbed in the city. The third time. The distance between that
and poetry is prime. Basement of number, or below that, some-
thing the foundation doesn't rest on. (Could we even see it? If there be
nothing under it. Is it all gap, then? Sheer beneath this shirt
or pen. Equally within. No primitive is narrative, if we mean by
that. What could the robber mean? To overflow the limbs, *limns that
limit him.* To do, get. Clarity and faith. An American
Hermes. Leading us to the end of story or the line wherein
we shall not look. Between each word or letter, then. Then back
to faith. Its origins. And daughters. That they let
men in. Narrow or ravenous beneath the skin. *What any of us
are inside of*, yes, and inside of us. A compass.

the week. Beneath numbers, what? "No narrative

is primitive. Who didn't say that? What's between nothing
and the first? Proceeds as from a stone at evening, released
from sky. Schoenberg's String Trio, con legno *bowing (both* battatu
and tratto) *and* sul ponticello *effect*–a musical thinker after a near
fatal heart attack. One glassy harmonic glancing off the
last. Mirror. Wherein the self (a *conjectural hypothesis
comparable to the existence of invisible light?*) peers into the vertigo
at the center of the eye. Éxtasis. As though you were your own
ancestor blazing from the serpent's jaw. Razor shadow on
the opposite wall. Congeries of what? Disappearances? Or flesh
speaking to the spirit (*that* device) of coming closer and leaving at
once. More and more like home and less. Of new complexities within
relationships long familiar. And the spirit attends. *That* poetry.

is natural (beneath time), a discourse, not a series

of events. What is it to see the body as it really is? Parenthesis?
Canvas of stars. Granite between the grain. If you lost your hands
you could never find them. This has been proven. Growing
straight or well forward. And a man rarely recognizes his own
profile. The infinite sentence begins, Life fluent even in wintriest
bronze . . . (What discourse is *not* event?) I can't feel anything but
my hands are breaking. Two rocks polarized in the desert like
Christ. Or a map of moles and scars beneath lamplight. Determinants
which define the situation and posit its value. Cars are running over
my entrails in the street! Something handed down from Upper Paleolithic,
no doubt, like handedness. Or in the predawn, a *piece of petalled
and delicate utility*. Dark membrane in the wind–influence between
the flashing of the world and the boundless brilliance beyond.

of events." I hear with my words, not really

mine. Is there a floor to being? And only one. Moon over
Wyoming. (Where I was all blowjob. Shaking at every-
thing. Spring. At fall. Where the first idea touched the face
of the void. *Nullam obicem ponere*. Stone floating in near
blue. Hammer. Petal. (*And delicate utility.*) Drawing forth.
Cochlea. Curved and small. (Do we see through the word
like time? Or in spite of it. Where passionate ear leads
passionate mind. The first time the world existed
in any sense discrete. Apart from flooding light and
motion. *Logos spermatikos*. Total reciprocity between the finite
and the infinite. Where new risen word in earthlight climbs
from eternal into indifferent blue. To which . . . Of
an oblique intelligence. Possessing and possest.

mine. How strange and true. As into a widening

gap. Depth beyond depth. And the word, *a bottomless*
pit. God in the emptying. As evening. Where the human more
becomes us. *Kenosis*. And the body, a span. Into the inherent
course of things. Between the tip of the thumb and little
finger. Between sound and *its* emptying. Not
a wall, but recurrence of motion through a *primal*
indeterminacy. Image a city boy in a country
of first things. *His* rhythm. Sky filling with darkness. Amber
face and hands. Bees in moonlight. A measure. Who? Of
what kind. *That which exists through itself.* Month, meal,
meat. *Is what is called meaning*. Now Juno, sister of Jupiter,
wife, through Old French, playing out through herself. As body,
word in its recurrence, emptying. Obedient to *its* end.

gap, metaphor and the basis of metaphor, *a* and *ox*, a sense

of loss plugged into an incommensurable. No common measure bearing a-
cross. Part outside of part. Hole in the sky. Blind o-
pening. How could it be otherwise? What unity with in-
difference? Nothing to take up, connect. How weigh the
attention of? Stretching toward, over, poised above
the abyss. *Experience of something that remains and is*
constant? Drawing forth. *Rills to suggest flickering*
movement. Under, up from under, over. Spring
of the ear. A fluid attentiveness. As though the world poised
over us. (Let nothing obstruct.) *I come from 36*
Union Square. Flowing between forms. The dream rustles the poet's
brush, alive to the analogous, where the heart lifts
and turns, dripping greens and reds . . . (To begin, commence

of proportion plugged into an unmeasurable," in-

creasingly fine sense of my own mortality. Imagine these words on a ledge
of infinite regression. Who would toss an oily rag on any
of them? Thin, slender. Of great care or delicacy. But
to die, be dead. What is that? Blooming in the desert. Cave
of all entrance. Creates this room?–walls, flesh. Sounding. *Everything
is accomplished through the senses.* Lip of light or
curve, through which . . . What is that rustling in
the darkness? Footfall. Voice. (Center whose circle is every-
where.) Of words, their registration. To bring back. Set
down. (Absolute in the scales of *resemblance and dis-
resemblance.* Of unknown origin. Yet possible at any time. Like
rain after drought. In the morning, insistence in each leaf or line. And
the word, saturated with light, half thought, half alive, returns.

cantation, faith or spell, "the transformation concepts

undergo, drawing words from a well, resurrection from root or
radio. Resurge from below. Watery associations. Waves heave
and source. A recurrence through. Now September across
the pond. Season dying in a rage of forms. To be reborn Saturday
night–in gloomy revery and readiness of eye. As on a staff or stake
of light. Night month, sixth day, seventh planet. (What
discourse is *not* magic? Flooding overnight, the dream rising,
ankles tied. (Whose feet, washed with tears, walks
this page? What world in capacious dark? Gone
over, returns. Luster, glance above the ardor of a poem. Last
Friday. Half a bone, torn eyelid . . . (No power that does not become
ear or eye. *Of rhythm is image*, etc. Construct. Of what we are. The. Wind
from the north, waters thick and cold, wrists in immaculate light.

undergo before magical discourse is possible.

Shift in categories, or difference in kind. An unease, general
and fragmentary, flows through the year's ruins. What remains
of the line. On ivory. Limestone. Radiance incising the edge, pen-
etrant. All those spines! And a density of intent bearing through an insistent
delicacy. Or rises like a filament in the wind. Silk thread. Glistens
in a silence of its own design, or strung with silences, dew on the web, fog
each morning. The heart at night. That would account the deepest
measure. Listens at the vault. Stars. And beneath the stars. Distant
pulse? What world, wet with elemental wonder, where we stood marking
the changes. Even then. Form into form. On liquid eye. Light trembling
in the vacancy. (What rises into being? Confluence of smoke and blood and
stone. As the heart, arc of attentions. Line. Desire without object. Without
remedy. Coltrane's feeling for *the hysteria of the times*. Goes out

the first concept before there was a concept,

drawing mind through being, in a disturbance of shadows, air
collapsing into air, the shifting edge of the indefinite, as over a fire, or
from the hawk's abyss, deepest recess of the song, "Don't Take
Your Love From Me." Algonquin. Iroquois. The wind has no
address. From in-the-midst. *A-letheia*. Neither the known nor un-
known. *Relaxation and dilatation of the heart cavities during
which the cavities are filled with blood.* (No event not pen-
etrant with the eternal. Blood filled with thought. A malignancy
of nymphs. Rock shore. Pulmonary blood. Ghost or joke
you'll never understand. *Lights the openness of the region
into which it comes*. Hot chambers of being. Nothing
beneath the skin. Nor whales, nor violins. Unbounding dark-
ness—*with the whole galaxy blowing up just to say something*

from *Fighting Kiwis*

The cumulus rises through declensions of summer's

heat toward a meaning subtle as the thirteenth
fingerbone of the violinist. Stadium lights
come alive before such grays and whites to argue
for the infinite. Thus Gregory of Nazianzus,
Whoso accepts the Theotokos shines with the light
of Godhead. Lovely. Likewise the landscape
wakes to such reflected light off cloudbank
that shadows stretch unfretted east to west
at sunset as if to claim that birth shall ever
follow death or that the spirit may contain
the uncontainable and be magnified thereby.
Mother of God. Even the Church, inert amid its vast
complacencies, at last agreed. Why not? Such music,
in the service of, lends an articulation to our lives
the greater as we drift into evening most holy, darkness
gathering in the branches, only the breath of light on grass.

Venus Hangover

Bless the hangman,
and bless his calculations.

Let there not be a knock upon the door,
And let me not rise to answer it.
Let no one be there,
And let her not be lovely,
  drawing me out into the dooryard, over
  the lawn, past neighborhoods, out
  of the city . . .

And let me not follow her into perfect Autumn
  where the last rose, beyond poetry, nods
  on its stem beneath the crow's echoing
  caw, and into sunlight, lacquered with thought,
  to follow the bee in her dance amid the flowers
  of attention and circumstance (her gambols
  would stump the sphinx!

And let me not follow her into a world without
  definition, infinity before meaning, beneath
  peaks of acetylene, drooping polymer chains,
  where the raw mind, howling and red, convulses
  before the naked face like a worm, a newborn
  left on a beach at the edge of a continent
  wherein we can never know the self nor
  even guess

And let her not lead me into night bulging
  with significance, a blind ocean of lamp
  shades and feet, eyeshadow and embalming
  wax, the delicate tap of the spider's fore

foot on the cheek, a sea of pure sound, pure
touch, the infinite loveliness of smell breaking
above us like memory–that great night,
luminous with doubt and self-loathing,
our egg tooth unsheathed, poised
against the dawn

And let her not take me up into the mountain
in the first spoors of light–that half the earth
remain hid, stars in the sky, and half revealed
in an extremis of white–as I cling to the cliff
with tiny claws, beyond fear, beating the bright
air of the spirit, my face at last decayed
by the purity of the wind, the corrosion of
desire, the acid of here and hereafter

And let her lead me not into *e*, zero
grade, where the first word, wound
of the world, cracks and reforms until,
crushed by water and rock, tree
and sky, it ruptures the throat to emerge, blood
soaked, squirming in its mucous sac, a curse
against the raven's cloak, the bat's immensities,
the hum of the corpse . . .

Let it hang there then
on its own damned stem between life
and death, jerking beneath the ruins of the sky,

And let someone else get up and stop
that damned knocking.

Spring Night

There are women who will undress
only in the dark.
– Creeley

Treefrogs in splendor. To inhabit the deepening
viabilities. In an agency of shadows, *high*
substance. Sound the interior of event. A-
mid the confluence. Shower of contingencies. Presence
amid the absences. State of being away, from. Yet
singularly engaged. (Light hangs on the scarp
of the Apennines. Emeralds in mediaeval dark--eyes
open gold on mountainside. *And men who will only*
surprise them there. To abide in a reverence to
the sources. That the whole include what is not, *theory*
of particular opacities. Shine over depth. Jeweled
breathing, open vault. And an enclave of clarities nesting
in lucid dream. Sustaining ravage. Darkness as

the *ground of light*. (What smell is not light? What
touch? *That* singular. And the wide sky. (How is it far
if you can think it? I have this vision of forms blowing up
like a silent movie inside. Limbs' wisdom lost. Least
sentience, web or trace across the surface. Going
out. Yet the delicacy of phenomenal insistence, this
night. Rods blossoming in starlight. Mars black
finish. Frogs. And beneath it all, a turning. River and
plow. Current through body, leaves, stars. To in-
quire of fullest need. Most urgent song. Shadow on
depth. Frogs' bearings, amplified. And the dance of elements
beneath the skin. Presence of no one, nothing, not to be
denied. Not touching her tonight. Not knowing.

How is it far if you can think it? What solace of

thought, ripe as body, light to touch, tenderness of
eye? As though a *solidity most spatial in its intent*
against the drifts and appearances that rise
and fall away in time. Province of a spring night. Or of
the world, its provenance. The whole articulating
matrix, between transitions of absence. Yet prior to gods
or man. Her flesh therein. Ivory inlaid with silence. Nimbus
in flux. Florescence. To attend the most intimate
connections. Complexities that blossom at the rim
of chaos. Eleusinian darkness, choric hymn. Earth again
in its rejoicings. Exceeds its origin. *Never more than*
at this moment. Through the matrix. Approaches, unfolds

Our crossing was a shadow
on darkness, a hot iron, the passage
of beasts. Deep in swell's pulse, we
sailed past the last vestiges
of memory, the detonation
of leaves, generation unto
generation, into a night, black
flame, darker than a dead man's
dream, the stench of burning feather
and flesh, cordite scoring
the lips, an acrid flame of dry
cement on the tongue, and on
the marges, electric surge
and collapse, the dissolution
of alternatives, sobs
in the lug, mounting the cranial
vault, and a dead rustling
on the hull, as we pushed through
the assemblage, stew of torso
and limb, gravegoods, resplendent
of genitals . . .
                                        And in our wake
on the lambent architecture of wave,
the ephemerata of the Ancient
Ones, where a hand still
twists, pointing,

You will never find it here. There
is nowhere else.

And out, onto the smoking
bank.

from *What Of* and *Adventures of Max and Maxine*

Max's Song

What could this be
the feeling of remembering
the causes in her face upbound as flowers now
as sleep now a florescence waking the peace
beneath the surface down to hands and
feet like headlights on a clown from which derive
the fortunes of the sky, silver encased, her face
the disquisition
What would this be
Would this be love
What of love and in its hour
What could this be
the memory of inside in-
side a sheath, within the nearest verities, enriched
neural weave–a casket blossoms!–her hand at the base
of my spine decried a radiance within the syntax of
the senses where even language is redeemed, the inner
arguments of verbs supplied, and words like letters living
pictures of speech, and where therein she brought me
to the emptiness of what happens
What would this be
Would this be love
What of love and in its hour
What could this be
could anything be more in-
volved than down here amid the loosening gravel
of thought without a metaphoric bed where she arrives un-
bidden enters the house in a fullness of light as
shadows beckon, Not everything will be
appeased, but of this one thing you can
be certain above all others as to yourself
be true, as though she sang beneath
distance

What would this be
Would this be love
What of love and in its hour
What could this be
the reinvention of an effect
by powers long exiled, without climate, attenuation of
the permeability between remembering and letting be, doors
of the heart and hand restless between two trees touching
a pond with a finger, looking back at our person from
beneath the surface, the face wavers
What would this be
Would this be love
What of love and in its hour
What could this be
stirring the water beneath the
dawn of chest and eyes, "a mere selvage woven upon
the fabric of wilderness," waking, picked up by the
sky, given to rain, to winds and breezes which so-
ever bind and in their binding run away
with my life
What would this be
Would this be love
What of love and in its hour
What could this be
the ghostly sheaths of cats, for
indeed they have a new grammar, as the residuum of an
odor, the peripheries alive in the smoke at the center now
lost in tributaries so long I wonder if it existed as though
I'd never seen nor heard nor did a single thing that was not
likewise informed by her presence
What would this be
Would this be love
What of love and in its hour
What could this be
the man who gave his life to live

with animals, that look in their eyes, as an orangutan's, listening
forms and shadows, he was convinced they know something
we don't, weight of sunlight in its seasons, parts of soul
contained in body, imperfect except they unfold, the artistry
beneath mortality, breath pouring out of flute, or as though
a woven song was only natural, melodia of voice and its
companion every morning of the world
                                        What would this be
                              Would this be love
                  What of love and in its hour

from *At That*

In the Short Term

– for Cindi

Life may be perfect, Ben Jonson
suggests, in the short term,
which is measure, you
were mine, no
more than perfection
is suggested
by any of this.

What Happens when Transparency Disappears

—wch we continue best to breathe by being unable thus to see
—Stephen Ellis

Oh, in my young youth I did not
care, the air itself was such energetic
matter, a battery of charges, as they
say, sought or seemed to seek or found
me, unaware, in an occasion to stay out, any
house, night drawing on, something
so damned curious even beneath street
lights as though it breathed and possibly

The transgression of Gaughin's left foot,
as if any choice was *not* toxic, that
we might take it for what it wasn't like
all this leakage of dream into a room
wherein the invisible universe surrounds
us mounted on wood over a wall in a
hole of ourselves

Struck down on the road to the ancient city,
monsters of air and flame pouring from skye's
engines, proto-linguistic signs punching away
at your liver, coming clear, the inner ball still
barely asleep in her eyes, the fervency of
night . . .
what is fire,
caught in opening
curtains

sic transit gloria mundi

Thus does the new moon lie cradled in earth-
light, intelligent and shy,
at
the nightly gathering, call it
a party, Jupiter and Saturn, attendant
strains singing in
procession,
stars entering
through a door in the east, leaving through a western door,
drunken wanderings of asteroids,
Orion rising midway
on his journey, song
on charmed
air,
epos, tales of glory, recensions and reticulations, deep
shine
–how will it sound on leaving? will
it echo in your being?–
'til morning breaks into
bud and bird like some nervous
reaction, I always wanted to write
about the resurrective powers of the world
so I have waited
'til my faith is waning.

Perhaps Romanticism *is* a system of habits as Burns suggests, not a series, does he sense a presence in that *system?* Waking to a silence as though someone has just spoken your name and is about to say something.

I was thinking this morning about transference and transformance in communication even when we hear ourselves, especially when we hear ourselves! *Surely thou shall not die*, sinuous baseline from beneath a luminant corner. Any word, say *natural* as a system of intertwining concepts moving like a colony of jellyfish or seaweed, as motion is given to all things living, each uniquely feeding and dying, yet each permeated with a presence, pull or longing across that gap which is what is meant by intelligence the word itself suggests, life

is preoccupation with itself, warm
rain Saturday afternoon, fields
running
to the horizon, ponds, trees stepped
in risen green, as presence to waking
dream amid such sleep as this
may be . . .

we are preoccupied

Surely thou shall not die, from the recesses, canyons, articulations of flesh and mind, sensuous reticulum enfolding hands and eyes, enveloping the senses, species knowledge, knowledge before that, as sound, what is it to know anything? and to be alive, as I was telling my students, even to a portion of what's going on at any moment can be almost all so borne of delight, why Kathy Acker drove a spike through her clit or shoved a vibrator up her cunt to write. I might not have a much of a future here, or anywhere I can imagine for that matter, yet everything seems to say, *sotto voce* singly and at once, antiphonal concrescence, caducean harmonic awash through the mind, this forgotten flower, *Surely thou shall not die.*

sic transit

sun and tree, field, brush, scrub, cattle, egrets, heron, pickups and cars, the highway
each morning rises
to the eye,
verdant, the daily
mystery of color,
its meditations,
vibrations, movement
of light to mind
the liquid streaming
lens or
edge
it is

preoccupied

sic transit

Congeries of beginnings each
morning, sun and birdsong pouring in
the mind's four
windows,
the soul
light from sleep rises
to coffee, new mown
hay, egrets following the tractor
for what
turns up, grass-
hoppers, cut
grubs, wounded,
given to light
torso and limb as
calculus of being

feel of your skin, taste of your mouth, smell of your body, bed and house is why outside is preferred, what makes death interesting

sic transit

Thus does the sun
rise beneath dragon shapes
cirrus pink
flames,
Chinese,
from which
quarter
also comes . . .

her face .

and I am drawn
to an integration
the implications of which . . .

hair, teeth, eyes, the relation
of cheekbone to cheek and between
these as an idea or something she sees
gives delight, remarks at, flashing . . .

crosses her face

world of cupboards
and streams, junctures of each
movement, moment
(where time has its being

Those rayes which all these flames
doe nourish

florescence of the limens
makes urgent the appetites,
the interstices liquescent

as though the soul doth so
inhabit . . .
indigenous
lambent

and unattainable.

sic transit

We who were alive, held you in arms, welcomed you to table, to
morning, the birth of distance and clouds, now ride toward an
interval, as though it were, terrain increasingly forward into which
we pass or cross or does it open to include us as . . . what?, one
of the hosts, lost to ourselves, the vast moving in and out of
being, as a dark mouth, aura of earth at 37,000 feet, to the east, nearly
seven miles, amid the towering brows of cumulonimbus, verticals seeped
in light, the *absolute structure of desire*, still yet moving, depth
rising from solitudes, passing as well into what opens to receive
us, all we ever hoped it was, despaired it might be, etc.

Light breaks above the darkness, holds the darkness, lifts off the fabric
of its disturbance, a haze, over stretching as though it were, sheathe
over memory, lights of towns and suburbs, nested in hills, flung
across the desert, above, another darkness, drained of all but
stars, the eye travels to whatever edge there is, hangs, falls
over or rises to the lip, cup or cusp, as though it were living, barest
shimmer over darkness, quickening, *the "not yet" diminishes as*
the concealing shadow disappears, abeyance of the provisional, rootlet,
tenthril, aviary in arborescence, dovetail, the emergent coming and
going at once, torso and eye, in transit, what would we know of it, or ask?

Night draws on darkness, unknowing caul, unsuspected because we
were suspended, an eye in its socket, slung in orbit over a blind
world, itself suspended within the conditional while the sheer
indefinite opens each moment beneath it, that there be an end
to it, whatever it was, distensions, business, the throbbing numbness
of limb or life while engines crawl ever deeper into a space beyond
the shadows we cast, were cast by, are yet contained, wherein we
led a life, were led in turn by others, and by existence itself
endlessly back to where we have come, no longer toward, space
without distance, where we wake to a voice, adrift in fetal dream

sic transit

Black
rot
in leaves,
country's negative, tissue of
mid summer
between days
of rain, weeks
of drought,

a proclamation of the dead,
coffee each
morning, other leaves
decayed desiccated yellow almost
white, birds in deep green, thread
of song & flight, cardinal
reel, mocking bird melody sewn through
arborescence, a grey-and-white cartoon, spring
widens into days
of summer, a primary
story implicit in the
chemistries of Earth it-
self woven into the present, three
morning doves across
the road, an owl some where as
heart
of alto flute,
another in the
north, hard
to say how far,
at a certain point response is
primary,
cattle bawl (what
for?), some

communication in
the pond, dace
shimmer, sunfish spawn, tallow
a brindled lace
in the middle distance, how
long?

sic transit

young sycamore turns on its side
before the storm, then light
rain

cars on the curve, sweet scent
of canted highway, wet
dust and grass, hint
of ozone,

coming to birth within the radical of what is
already
plethora, I thought last night
falling asleep, the rain so
insistent and the cars in their ratios

of innocence, measure moving as
well, round the curve, trying
to get elsewhere, not otherwise, as
panacea
for the stench of existence,

yet deep breathing of all the senses sustains me in
the belief, rising, that the world is born in and through
us, each
an umbilicus, tender
conduit for
thought
as fluid tissue within which sustenance
we feed its fetal
dreams,
that we

might find the world elsewhere or otherwise
conceived,
I sit and listen,

. . . wasp slapping
pheromones on cypress post, hieroglyph
of deepening code,
mechanics of spring brought to summer's
vast engine

velvet black cross as lace,
malignancy in the heart of
summer, fringed rot, what
is birdsong except
a redundancy of sleeves, perhaps eyes
in the words themselves, fungal
spots, fairy rings round septic
tank, clouds in high
light

before storm

cicada
again as
memory of exchange, echo and audible
swell, ages
past, over three hundred yards a-
part, between risings of
wind and breeze, sound
riding beneath distant
thunder several thousand feet a-
way, over two miles, I can't see the
lightning, the Renaissance
mocking bird is at it again, but you
can tell he's listening as well, two
vans and a pickup, a medium
size luxury car, and a small bare
bones white sedan drive by
while I write this, a bell sounds
in the distance
like it means something (headline of the
gods?), more cars and thunder more
birds, cicada suddenly
quiet, they
themselves
are an idea

after storm (sic transit)

branch dripping and root
dripping consciousness
as cicada's juice otherwise rises through
conduits of the crepuscular, lucent as fungus, virus
as vibrant, a vibrance to shake a-
part vibrance, a mind, fins nose
pond's surface, for what answer *is*, but the dying of
questions, few birds in the sky, torque of newt
and gecko, deep eye-blink, milk white,
a mosquito raises once again its tongue
into the air, into spaces of the air
–where carbon dioxide triggers receptors as surely as
as the aroma of steak . . .
then these open, eyes
& legs, shake,
rise again to vision
from where they went in rain, beneath leaf,
dirt, water, moss, and mushroom the cartoons
would have it, or as though a place a-
part (Old Earth looks at us, puzzled
& amused, Haven't you a clue?) . . .

these the living
after storm has passed, shimmer at each
edge, blind dripping of eyes other-
wise rises to gauze
of existence
this evening

Economics of Metonymy: sic transit

Matrix alive in limb, pseudopod, tenthril, voice
with eyes' eruction, light pouring down for days, lonely
voice lost in its own century, Where have you been?
To lose the voice is to lose the self, weightless lyrical orb
tugging the vinculum in space, depthless, amniotic, wakes
from vowel-soaked dreams, plunges onto morning's
talus, coughing bricks of fur and small bones, You've
been at it again (jizzed-on tits, your toe-nails painted to match
your favorite dildo, shreds of crinoline in your stool). Homer lost
in a voice over 400 years, aspirant wandering whirlwind of
elements, cicadan thwirl, sibilance wrapped in gases, adrift
on glissandos waving in the mesh, rising, falling off, over
as a cliff, into deep summer, echo in eyeless dark.

Matrix of vein in leaf, in leaves, surge and resurgent, forth and
back, as rivers flow forward yet turning ever seek their
source, like the heart, its founding waters. Pathetic and
lovely to watch a man discover his own mortality. Winds
die into breezes, breezes along walls where he wakes,
alone. A strut loose in his eyes, the hemorrhage of referents,
recognition, he knows, as do few, the utter truth. Darkness
beneath the sky, or beyond in summer, the infinite rising
and passing away which itself neither rises nor passes. Last
night I dreamed of a communal bathroom for the faculty,
sweating shithole in lounge filled with people you wish
you didn't know and where there were also baskets
of chocolate, fragrant, amelt. Promises, promises.

Light turning the corner into thicket, breakfast and sex
leaking from pores, matrix of season as form, boundaries
fluid, spilling like eyes or mushrooms in and out, morning
sun on desk instead of battle, socks and shirt, talk rubbing its
genitals on my leg, whereas eyes as *the stem of brain touches*

light rose on highway's bright abyss, mounted as sunrise (Hath not the highest chambers of my being rang with song?), mind a-wash in color, as world, the balm on her eyes lead her to hallucinate a blind man who beckoned her to hell, or the light of anticipation that shook with you as you waited in line to fuck your sister, *the way goeth, or leadeth hither, or thither,* cream on dirty fingers held to windows or mind, as though you could so arrange to be the displacement of either.

Matrix of contiguities, polar and blind, as is future. *Whereas ways cannot go nor proverbs speak.* Silence of language passed over in science. Airy spaces within sounds, letters, words, between letters and words more spaces, systolic and diastolic silences, aphasic abyss in each moment, distension of oblivion in paragraphs, margins, all the talk of worlds. Road stretches across morning, time and space. Matrix of contiguities, limbs and eyes taking form, stiffening, crowded out of emptiness, where anything comes from. Cancer is eating at a friend. I don't know which one. I will soon enough. Polar and blind. Silence *is* the future. Once Silence came from the Woods of the Future and sat down and began to talk and so on. It was his heart in the words . . . (ask Borges). An edge on the silence that it might be heard . . . (ask Spicer). The most puerile excuse for juvenile ardor, ask your sister. No thing not so much in words, the old joke, nor in the world as well.

Motion is the grammar of forms, of which death is answer. Declensions of color, shape, and movement. Tree and sky for calibration, the entrance and exit of the phenomenal almost simultaneous, not quite, recognition of the nameless in the named, of such is body. Colors float across the eye, woven in the visual cortex to their shapes, which is of essence (a question), and motion, boat drawn across water and evening give rise or words through black holes of intracranial space suddenly appear, *locus observandi*, like the intersections of trees in dream. Echolalia of worlds within words, where anything rhymes, like the nausea of its own condition you can't get away from in a redaction for heaven, one of our assumptions has always been it may be the same going in and out of bodies, we've forgotten. The mint on the pillow is for when the animal sacrifices are over and you're trying not to smoke.

sic transit

Kingfisher in highest cypress green
against ciel,
across which pass
three egrets, weaving
tiers of this world, sight
and sound, screen of heat
on feather and skin,
hide and cypress
bough, ply upon ply,
they will be passing all
day, back and forth through
the mesh, field
unto field, fishing . . .
the congress
of being, grasshoppers, grubs, what-
ever passes *through* these blades
of late summer mowing, chort
of cardinal driven
from field, mocking
bird more temperate in
conversation, cicadan
drift . . .
the frogs silent, cough
of green heron, a different room
each time, pauses lovely
to contemplate

For by death has been wrought
greater change
than hath been shown.

shudder of light in breeze, dragon-
fly

at that

A stranger stands in front of your car, you put him
there or the dream did through the divine agency of
poetry you write in sleep, he is obstruction, rhyme,
throws us back into a field, it doesn't matter of
what, what of, or is all matter, what anyone wants just
words across a field or felt of ice, cards in slow
motion, or sparrows over the road where I would be
going. I stopped, I knew I would forget, the phrases
melting into lines and words running to wild heather,
a blind daughter, the logic so pure I *would* remember, I
thought, a lake in the mountains, how it breaks back on
itself, fresh as a broken branch or last night's repetitions
of creek, bed amid flora, fern or words watering rock.

Economics of Metonymy

Eyes installed in sight, blindness of orbit, these leaves
are blackened ground, shine with a rosary in remembrance of
dreams, trees as hammock of eye as well in orbit, dew falling
from highest branches, fern, time and morning, to ear. Motion
as transubstantiation of time into form, cause an intent carved
into the grammar of space. *All things shall be accomplished
through the senses*, and so forth, a prophet forgetting where
he left his cart, the slaughter of each our daughters before
the night is too advanced. Death had always seemed an
illustrated letter at the opening of a fairy tale, happily
tangled in magic. Naked father turns to naked daughter, "It's
okay, Darlin', it's what daddies and darlin's always do after
spankings." Objects rushing to the center so absorbed.
Depth of force in magnet. What life goes begging?

sic transit

Darkness folds back from
darkness, more
darkness, skin over
skull, un-
folding, mind's evaginations,
valley
of stars in the sky,
silence of
cities below,
ephemeral
haze of light off face in
window, dream and the
beginnings
of dream, as we bank slowly
south . . .
lightning in the distance, as
though explosions on the cusp
of creation
–everything leaving and entering
at once,
passing
through . . .
yet the heart trembles
at its door,   darkness of blood not yet
gone
over stands eager though ever un-

sure, as though returning to what never
was, what we never
were, in this way (only?) similar to
existence, the inter-penetration
nearly complete, engines swelling
into nothingness, transparencies
dissolving, layer
by layer

Economics of Metonymy

Bronze by gold heard the hoofirons steelyringing.
- Joyce

Balancing as metal, its sound, the metal in its sound, itself bright, balanced with preposition, riding the syllables through words of streets, sounds off paving stone and buildings, apace yet with deliberation, as is its kind, sounds as crowds in streets to hold them off, sound of metal in its sound as abeyance is off bright walls of sound, though often dim, the sound to bounce walls off, unlike Balzac-the need for song is free though its fee's unpaid-it sounds like someone, a wooden leg, stands up in its occupation of being sound, something he'd rather do than not though he realizes its bright absurdity also has a sound which is as discordant as well as abeyant, *bronze by gold* as bright hair is known by beholders everywhere and nowhere such metals are, and such hair, it's a matter of communion. Sound is a grammar of motion as well as forms, a horse through the Dublin streets, viceregal hoofs, and so forth before even Homer there were men Jaynes tells us who heard voices streaming through the air like hot milk, like blowing out a blind man. If you think you're seeing something, you think you're seeing something. Everything is certain, a head falls from the hand like the skull of Mary. The universe is out of order.

Mad to Be Wed

–antidote for an epithalamium
for Micah and Sunnylyn

Word behind bars keeps hitting its wall on
the head while mind starts a riot in the food
line, soon we'll all be back in our cells eating
grubs, chaos ringing in the diencephalon. Life
after life spread like lye or lime over bodies, spread
like syphilis, the luminous kind, that loosens
tongue and eye, then watches the body from another
room as it fades into an narrative old as the orb
itself new made each morning, the ripe comedy of
an existence with an iron bar driven through the
parietals or the white flame of a blowtorch held
to the temporal bone, upper right. Old joke, too
real. See how borrowed photons from the moon
illumine the skull from beneath and behind, how
supple their play amid sutures, across occipital
plains? Kaput. Listen, I'll kick you in the
head, if you'll kick me in the head. O.k.? Here,
stick this up your cunt. Here, let me fix your
prick. (There is a mountain large as thought
where you can go sometime, be forever, but with
another of your kind, how? How do we do it? How
might it be done? I leave this to you and yours.

Wagon-lit

–for Tom Clark

To lie, lay, night lit, to light a word, small
flame, and carry it as woman's face the world
varies all night in dream amid the shattering, four
monkeys like bats with nets catching insects or
some-mores, small flying reptiles with organs
sweet as dried fruit above trees, clarinets with
uncles, wise beard as well as can be well expected
to turn on the edge like black sedge is beard or bird al-
so monkeys where what was looking in (i.e.,
nothing), or what was it heard, of, is in just
contention with what *is*, as if to imagine such
a word is to live in its sounding, bell or body,
where what lights it lies down beside you in
the dark, matter the night, matter the wind.

sic transit

Neither does the world answer but
in mute response. Cold
wind this morning before
dawn, cold
rock in its eye,
frozen
dream in its mind. All
things are drawn to distraction. Evening
loses itself in night as Venus
rises
into softest flesh,
blue above white, mere
yellow, which thighs are pillars of this
world, that they might break and
tumble in time.
Moon rises
between Jupiter and Saturn, who
turns that we
might see her rings,
thinnest structure yet observed in
nature,* she paints
her nails to match the furthest
colors of the universe, gold, ocher,
heart in ice.

* *A fifty-story building stretched across fifty-continents the size of North America, if that helps.*

Mind responds, Deep
Wanderers, crossing and re-
crossing the mystical band, arc or
sash, narrative as fluid tissue, shore,
endlessly
searching, for so it
seems, each sign a station pronounced
sentence or dance of mythos, fluent,
within
what?

from *For To*

sic transit

breeze over dayspring   out
the window   what is the body of
trees but leaves   pulling to the south   re-
lax northward,   in waves   the elemental set into
the elemental,   blue beaten thin   to light
orange   due east   dusty blue on the treeline
and I'm wondering about prepositions . . .

later,
dance of window pane and chair on
carpet,   wind rising   in chambers of air
stuttering frame of shadows   as worlds,   shuttle's
reticulations into morning   narrative of which
we'll never know the end

Griddle of the Inexorable

–for Stephen Ellis, a triangulation

It's hard to tell if what she showed you was a three-pronged dildo or television, attenuation of desire at any rate, maybe the head she bit off in the Conception Gallery, watering thongs and cogs, strapons, bushings, gears and belts with the blood of whatever preys on midnight's machinery as all but thought came crashing to a halt, moving parts spilling off and into a forest of signs, syllables, the world of words, tales, lakes, rumors of caves beneath water, wavering light of room. Can you pin it down, the moon? Glorious aperture. What then of self's griddle, girdled to torso, stench of feather, fermenting meat, burning hair, bone gives metal to smoke, *all our living effort* to meal, the gristle of what it is to remember, magnification through speed itself, body of desire driven into distances from which position *and* momentum, the "weight" by which an object itself exists undeterred by a universe of mutually exclusives, yet through the agency of *the closest twin to life there is*, is made manifest, bounds back in light as through another body.

Birdsong

honeysuckle, sight scent and
touch, fingers eyes nose slipping
into oblivion of blossom,   and a taste
of ozone . . . (way back, where yet the five senses
dance in a ring,   in an inner chamber, half
filled with lake, of the diencephalon, before
the screen goes blank . . .

the approaching storm

silence of
birds
& wind risen to whatever Earth
says
when we listen,

All is inconstant, existence in
drift, something like the remission
of nothingness, not
quite, but as temporary as any
mind you could posit
life you might
bear

title in bold

I mean *that* as a hole someone's begun drilling through the mountain, a few cracks with the stick: granite cliff to talus, light shines on new rock, new demon in echo, resounding word, its iteration on air shimmers, charged and recharged forever though at times it is a crevice, in the evening, natural enclave wrought by ice, frozen brow cracking up over fifty-thousand-year-old processes, which is to say what? That we find whatever we find in their presence, even our own recognitions, or as others look in as well, communion driving past such ruptures of vision, hooked in sight-stream, a liquid take, spell pouring past in granite, measure we look at, then set it back, next to its idea in a forest of referentials, noting its kind *and* the juxtapositions, configurations, whatever we can, the exact light on the cactus as sun disappears over canyon's rim, how it's no joke, turning it on the shelf, hard edge of rock, how swift and brutal the necessities. Wasted life.

"Who ya talking to?"

-Travis Bickle

What kinda integration is it can't stand itself?
This time the Donner party's vegetarian and asks
for smoking. Hunger feeds on hunger smothered
in desire and dreams of something other than an-
other connection in the claustrophobia of its own
condition. Insert clatter of kitchen, dishes,
and scents that slice thru the same olfactories
with the same results for millions of years (roast
human?) over a table of their desire, corner
window and wall on which a picture of mountains
echoes with melodies recalling them home-
ward like Tamsen's last dream of another century
where *all* the passes are closed though restaurants
stand open 24-7, like truck stops, *everyone* wired.

Solstice nearly three weeks out

sparks the ripeness of fire blood speaks to the mind of a knife like a sharp nose searching backwater towns for missing children, there's talk about crying, some nights, just up from Old Wharf, it derives its sweetness like a life mislaid, set aside or aggressively fucked, dipped in honey and staked out in the heart of *something fierce*, yet a softness for all that. Who hungers in the darkness?, what hunger in voices lost like the opposite of cricket is . . . what? Where had I heard those buoys before? On what coastline? At whose house? or was it a dream like a movie tucked in a drawer, a mystery lifted from the forties, that is a clean mind and heart, perhaps haunted by loss or guilt yet potentially still pure, are suddenly confronted with an evil neither could have guessed on its own nor they in their conjunction might have imagined, in fact it took the world to conceive, waking beneath moon smudge in fog beside the nude body of a child, the grasses wet with our excess. Buoys in the distance, sobs in the pauses. This is the first I'd heard.

Ah wonderful rare wilderness the blank page

echoes, as a shadow echoes off canyon
walls where it sails across the valley floor to echo
in the heart of language, itself interpenetrant,
interwoven, dissolved as the moon, resident
of night, rises, makes meditant the fierce
darkness, falls on stoned interiors, wave's
shadow rolling over valley all night, clouds
rising up mountain to fall again in day-
spring, given its lightness (can you hear
it?) as form rises into the formlessness of
dawn, then over the edge into the future, its
echo as well as its shadow reflected,
god metal planet plant, in every word

sic transit

face after face   enters the screen   life
after life   rises   beckons   into the swirl
bright glitter   awash in light   ply
over ply   and so forth   the hand in the
eye   pauses   a silence of sight   in
the vortex   sky's reflection   on water
green empathy   of trees   cicada   white
heron   against cumulus   massive floating
anvil   gray blue   as a thought
shimmers in light   over pond's   grammar
bullfrog   thrush   that but for us   there
are no verbs   in nature   no run runs
plumb   nor treeline   but curves   the
smallest fly   an intelligence   to be reckoned

from *Tongue*

And the power to tell is glory

The tongue is the largest organ of the body, just ask the moon
or the homunculus who operates it, thumb up his butt, fish
dying in mouth for want
of water, lily in glass case, or tenthril set
to air
floret,
small flame,
that
by which we are most known
yet
dumb to tell . . .

the story runs out like a relief pitcher,
overanxious (glorious youth!), to
the mound. (He doesn't know
it yet, but he'll never be able
to forget what
was about
to happen.
The pillow, itself,
will become a tongue, and
the room . . .

will tell of it, stupidly,
repeatedly . . .

toll
of the heart.

from *Tongue*

whatever happened?
how speak of it, that which is yet,
perhaps, in its earliest infancy, shelf of shore
breeding a continent, interior even farther than *we'd*
conceived, ever, or had we? It sometimes seems as though
we'd always known it, that an organism or an array of such inner-
responsive reactions to the common condition would be thus harmonic
or of a progression in which we might recognize an intelligence, like a man
in the words, at least briefly, sound in the understanding such as rocks are
hard, and stone, in its conception, a mountain beneath the lake, of what
is it to tell?

from *Tongue*

fire (borne) fragments of bone shards of
paint pots grave
goods foot prints

or decaying mounds of skeletons, oily
sludge *of what*
was once at least twenty
individuals saturated with
the glossolalia of dreamspirit, thousands
of years, the cave it-
self whispers, corruption
seed or

a
bear's skull
set on block
of stone
overhanging
jaw,
tongue and word as well
as world,

points to The Bear Gallery

the cave whispers
to itself

nec mortale sonans

from *Tongue*

A drift in the tongue

Invisible architectures of tongue, vasculatures of dream, a devastatingly brilliant series of dry executions, its cycles synchronize all of mind's correspondence to the sacred lunar phases, self-correcting for azamuthal variation, a clock set for spontaneous combustion, otherwise the light of the moon would strike the tongue so seldom that any relationship would be negligible. Like ambient poetry. See what I mean? It is the mind's *thumb*, can grasp, as a tool, or that *other* instrument, also bridled, brings torque to world, twist of diphthong to declaration, annihilation of entire populations, harangues, blubbering confessions, and almost unspeakable lusts. The opposable tongue. Of all nature's organs, the most variable, at least in terms of weight, this gives it density in our consideration, or is it weightless, floating through a gallery, all one Rauschenberg, continuous areas of conjunctions, his mind in folds, and on the floor and ceiling it continues until you realize that you might not even be inside any more

It's really odd

I'd not miss it for the world nor would I give the world for it. Fortunately, I don't have to. That's where you come in. This could be a love poem beneath a basket of skies. Say, I want to speak to someone about a leak. It's really a hemorrhage, leaching the vital fluids of words into the world, what's left of it is hung out like a dead pet to dry. This language is broken playground equipment. Seizure of monkeys in the carpet. Cat as death trap, neural paralysis of fleas, oblivion's hose, or the *vacancy* in *vacuum*. Hello, "Tear me off some." It's 5:15 a.m. "Goodbye, My Beloveds," Gorky's last work, white chalk on painting crate. I could suspend it from the beam in my living room. Abstraction as the "experimental inspection of the hitherto unknown."

Cicada in the near distance,
in the far distance, in
the differentials,
glimmer's number,
pond
shimmer, scum, pollen, smallest
thrush, a bull frog, and I'm
occasionally coughing, bulldozer
a few properties away
tearing the earth a new one all
over again, and
crickets, of
course, I can hear the horse shudder,
insects passing my ear, cars
on the curve, rusty hinge
of bird in the field, cricket
frogs again, . . . once they
opened a door and I
walked in. It
seemed simple.

still does

Sonnet

three isochromatic triangles stacked and perched on a tiny
foot over ground speeding past or two lumbering fellows in a
boxcar sharing a broad and a smoke and then getting into it
fur flies somebody dies before the end of fourteen lines more
or less yet I always wonder why *its* extensible intent should be
so prevalent, fertile as two fairies goosing a wee child they tied
down & are riding to town on a Saturday night no one will want
to ever remember like the shimmering sense I left the flame-
thrower on at home in fact I *am* a bit flushed & feeling packed
up & untrussed all over like loosening wet howls in my jacket
(sorry) my dick's on backwards again or badly hanging out on
purpose into the stew of polite clauses pay it attention and it
will pay attention to you what's so reciprocal it can't wait until
morning or find completion driving into evening like the sea?

Distant thunder, abiding rest, mid-morning, which I
think it is ten, rings of pond scum, brown and velvet at
once amid green and white reflections, formed by
breeze rising to wind, arc of attentions rides across para-
bola of late summer, cicadan pulse, as an18-wheeler *rounds
the bend* until, I guess, a circle is *realized,* a machine that
can self-replicate, endlessly, needlessly, like a word, it
must have had its source in the sun, or so we think.

Clouds darken in the northeast, mediation of color by
color as form passes into form, there is no such as one, the
sole, discriminate, that does not move toward many, none
that is not permeated, does not return, then outward and
again that every movement may be realized in accord of
which each instance is utterance of fact (It's going to
rain), simply, and that everything you've learned may
come to nothing, but for the largesse of such moments.

Flood of color deepens as trees are again persuaded down-
ward and to the left, northwest under daughters' dark
healing, come what may, (clouds? . . . it *is* that simple, yet
in the complexity of its address there breathes a sense of presence
(only?), as the palm in the mind *is* a tongue, which is also of
material substance, like the heart (and that intricate, now that
the relative has been restored to include what the eye follows or
in thumb's ear where pears are falling as circles pattern pond.

Abattoir of Desires

–for Brian

tongue as measure	wedge of what depth	strung with eyes brachiation	proportionate to flesh
wedge of what depth	inches forward by conjecture,	swings or lopes, pole	to point whereof the mind is
strung with eyes' brachiation	swings or lopes, pole	to toll endlessly of the heart	given to another and again until
proportionate to flesh	to point whereof the mind is	given to another and again until	swallowed in her sounding...

Nothing Is Final

- for Bill, his fiftieth

and inside the card: Which is nearly true enough, as such things go, almost quite literally, or at least nominally so, dig? (I.e., some people *don't* pay taxes, and *I* for one have never died.) Now of *your* "three-score years and ten," *fifty* will never come again. But the hell with Houseman. His picnic, stuffed with flowers, turned into an early wake where we ran from the downpour, found a barn, shook ourselves off, and fucked like corpses. So relax, as they say, it never the fuck was going to be alright anyway. We can *leap* or *be given* to flames (how strange that *given*, as though someone's been eating at your table you don't know, or your son gives you a look where you can see the universe sliding by beneath, etc., and you're caught once again wondering if life is too short, or too long. Neither in hope nor despair. I mean you're just wondering, right? Best wishes.

from *Thumb*

Preface

A thumb for the gouging of eyes, or imperative, descending end of pliers for pulling tongues. Thumb for Pendergast (you'd have to know him) and his marbles' (which would mean to spank him) prophetic spin (soundly) like galaxies, only bigger (each dawn, every day, for the rest of his life. Dumb messenger. A thumb for the portals of furthest cast rhythms, rhymes deeply won. Are these simply words, and what might *that* mean in a capital sentence of digits? Always a thumb in the ground of the serious (but is it bearing down? or a presence beyond its youth, in use. How could we know, and what might *that* mean, and again? No question of whatever's evoked in the name of all *I* know and of its nature, the thumb has its hand in it.

from *Thumb*

Of What Is Purchase?

Most contemplated appendage. Thus we model
our mind, or on our stomach, cock or cunt, hairline,
nose, cheek's relation to the *memory* of cheek, touch,
simply,
how the mind folds into time, prods the earth in its search,
continual, for foundation, and with such instrument, the very
architecture of which represents, in the cleanliness of its line, such
intent. Fuse of the world, of mind the measure, extension. Grant me
the Song of Putting Down the Hammer On.
All Our Dreams are commonly staged on the thumb, but
it's also a set so vast we don't recognize it and think we are back
in our own houses or in the houses of our youth, where something
might yet exist, or back in the hospital, or in the hood getting
really messed up (*Gonna get fucked up awful bad in just
about ten seconds!*) What
life sprouts on the thumb? Might it exist
without? Wobbling center, it gives us
us purchase, in ordinate in even amount like
that unresponsive man, or series of accretions he calls
intelligence, thinking he really thinks before he says something
Such men are thumb
deficient. Delusion in just
proportion to their distensions, to which the hand
gives evidence. Dumb propeller, mind's foot and
so forth. What is it to be so alone? The thumb
knows, shuffles the stars, laughs out of
turn, any turn, the concept of
turn torn from an incandescent box of forms, and pushes on

from *Thumb*

"So little's given us, why pity less?"

Or envy more? Thus, the god we inhabit banishes
scale under banner of justice-being-what-it-is as
world, what we would *with* it, what world we would,
would we have? *Now get off your horse.* Proved more
than dangerous in little time. Standish out of Massod, al-
Qaeda, a wannabe gansta' with the public will (a
determined somnambulism) "strongly" behind him,
Ashcroft sweeping across vast stretches in furious blind
pursuit of his own inadequacies, dark loathing, dread
beneath the lines.
                                        What land? Whose?

But even his *sense* of his own confusion is uncertain,
vague (*Where's this mad fucking hatred coming
from?*), his faculties solidified into that which other-
wise would be known as an identity, the human, not
this excremental stalagmite cold torched like iron
to cave floor, in short someone to whom we are *meant* to
show deference, if only that his protestations seemed to
convince *him*, him*self*, that his vacuities were covered
in ways we knew ours never, to satisfaction, were. Thus
we were given the vote and *the act* at the same historical
moment. In a few thousand years ol' Numb Nuts will be
going out each morning of his life to add another pelt
to his corporate belt, actually a toupee collection (he
keeps them on his desk, center spike).

                                        So little's given us, go
                                                take a fucking hike!

Our crusty world breaks at my feet like lobsters and
crabs with chilled white, service til dawn. The orgasm

sweeps across both hemispheres with its little sleeping feet releasing orgone at every step (where sky's orange comes from), in a ballet of existence, entering a state where mists, hugging the surface, brighten even as they slide off into deepest space, to entail the stars. What molecule gone up, forever deferred, the sweet juice that never reaches gut of satisfaction but that there is not, in such sweetness, a fatality, the presence of all we have lost, are losing, can anticipate ourselves in the absence of. This is the name of the most difficult in several incarnations.

They had not yet left the ships, in fact, when Standish began ripping off the local populus, *a breed just below the Spanish cur, these things are meant to slide by on their bellies, anyway, it's good fortune nobody's here*, *the only truth is in my hand*, echoes the heart the head, distance called lost (Whose land? What caves?) *Man's natural state IS darkness, And the sooner you realize THAT, the sooner you'll take that joint outta your mouth and help us develop calibrations for the NOTION of lethality based on the stratification of radical dispersals, at once supple AND nuanced! Dig?* Only error's margin keeps us alive any moment to the next. By this, I mean nothing fancy, breathing as though you've done it all your life, matching your intent to theirs, notching it up.

The design at once so grand and meagre that the sheer scale of its indifferentiation is dazzling, looking down, what *could* they have been thinking, raising such towers into such a sky? The state of Texas, one *big* motherfucking thumb, zero minus one, a dimension both vast and vague (i.e., there's little room in all that space) yet with an edge that'll open bone on the first pass, or when it rises, sun over sill of such a world with the mind of a machine, it will tend to make you re-calibrate your response, before proceeding, . . . straight on.

Cut twice, *then* measure.

So *much* is given. He who says otherwise belies the human, reveals his life for the shabby dissemblance it is, the glint in his eye all abdication all the time, 24-7, until he thought *this* is what he'd read about and dreamed about, adult existence, sadly toxic, a quiet dance in the enervating drift we know as contemporary culture, life, what do I care?, but never the measure, thumb as jewel in hand, something for the pen or brush or wand instead of a neck. Something for the hammer and dick for Christ's sake! Star in its socket, the hand's grave, rhymes with prophet who proceeds *I am he in whose forest there is great need, confusion the master, columns of petrified trees, eyes swinging from god to god.* The mind's socket, obsidian, mirrors the hand's, but *its* jewel cannot so easily be discerned.

from "Scroll: Stars, Clouds, Earth"

world turns
on water
waters beneath the leaves

showers of meteors beneath
waters

jeweled beginnings
rare openings
(etc.)
ringing in the ears

at night, the famous anthology

Arcturus, Horsehead,

Orion cradled in the young maple

(it's late, winter . . .

the Leonids cross mind's canvas,
each pass a
pulse, brushstroke, welling of
silence across the deepening vault, an
idea, thought, speck
of dust

(that which is enduring, endures, even in the arms
of the transient,
most fickle tree

How does it start?
Where is the beginning?

Can anything be lost?

looking through the socket of a missing eye to
search the world in its blindness,

a thought
floats on these waters,
as mind on leaf,
that we are the

suspension of that which does not exist,
the occlusion of nothing, *na*-, without extent

which goes neither
one way nor
the other & of which there is no
desire, nor distinction

but is its own satisfaction, and
except
for that little twitch toward existence, would be
entire

•

How is it then, of it made, more of it than it is? Simonize the
street, go long in discretionary options, short on light, break
right, try for center. I'll meet you there. Etc. A twig, not
even a thought, nor anything of which to speak, I'd rather
not say amid these presences (clouds), the address of which is
silence in towering heights,
selvage, banks of light pouring down
mornings of a life (disappearing
scale) through heaven's crevasses, deep rivers of
sky, mediate loneliness, dominion's corrugation, cloud's

surface full of seas, mind on display, god in
inmost cortex . . .
below,
water
meanders, turns
on itself, coils, cuts it-
self off, another
dinosaur carved into the delta of lost
rivers, towns, lives abrupt, yet absent voice the mind is a
grid graven on such fields, graph, I guess it makes sense but
from where I sit, amid this gathering, gallery, it looks thin within
what-
ever luster man might have eyes on, birth of
wonder, dead accuracy of the real, hard
acknowledgment even this, set amid these
presences, as though within the given (winds out
of the west) as supplicants approach the bench, one
prophet among them and
they *all* become prophetic, gods' wide appeal as
mind in ear opens, morning's lost cause given to
bright turbulence of spirit, melody in mind's cavern, the return
of distances, sheathes gathering beneath over-
hanging shelf, tidal pull of clouds none
can calculate save that he who cannot
believe cannot live does not mean
anything's the case, what we'd will, yet in
its realization is a language which constitutes the given across
a sky never written but recognized, scouring light, the weak eye
wanders, wonders, what is it that is actual, here, in resemblance
of conception as identity sailing over the abyss from one silence
to the next across ear's distances in mind of hearing . . .

or what would we have that we so listen might thus approach
when we are ready at last for the absence of which we may
be its only response only its response could I tell I would,

and as closely   as your nighest name,   wife waking
you up   to what night will,   then,   have of
love   room beneath storm   rain and
thunder   flesh to cherish at
hand, palms' encumbrance
as senses are
stripped from earth's
body   gratuities over-
flow the cup,   bowl,   basin of
stone   and all the reservoirs are over-
flown,   who could so imagine it otherwise   would
approach with like reverence,   look into its liquid heart   sound re-
semblance for   chord of deep response   harmony of which   even if it
be but correspondence between that which exists   and that which
we find ourselves among   only clouds can calculate   such
meaning,   what is it of the heart   that finds it-
self otherwise   wrought of phenomena

rather a room   a lantern   within a storm
a silent man who speaks   a dog that
listens   logorrheic absences of sound   'mid
mind's evaginations: future time, past present,   the world *is*
porous,   and who might hear   with like ear   would realize
water itself is of the measure   and clouds   faith in recognition   mind
in being   *through* which the nonexistent is revealed   in its quotidian
concretion   *in accordance with the tendency to falling*   *essential*
to everydayness   waking as a series of recoveries   adrift in the
third chamber of the heart listening, always   for an echo   ourselves,
in what we are a part   what are the odds   that anyone should care
to listen   pierces!   in the act the apprehension,   noun always
embedded in verb   verb infested with noun,   and yet we seek
a presence   within that manifestation   streets of the world   neither
darkened aspect   nor *pearly spouse*   but of its own insistence
transparent to itself   answer to its only question   absolute   pure
appearance, man who drowned in the object   writing Days of a Life

Form,   the mighty Mississip   flowing backward   into the rift
of New Madrid, or he who, lost in self's roar, gives testament of nearby
falls, or maybe eyes like my father's   look into the other room, with
neither hope nor despair   *nil admirari*   as though the zodiac were
woven into our bodies rather than this failure   rising from a mis-
conception,   not accidental,   not unsubstantial,   an *increasingly*
hardened forgetfulness of being   "constrained"   to the narrative, to
play it out   we, who never signed a contract   though we would
have   gladly and   perhaps, with some revision   would do
so again   (but this time put ourselves   at least in the way of
understanding,   have now come to an end   the first? (what
have we forgotten?   has forgotten us   dealt us last   in our
passing?   that we would listen,   the ear is also mute   as
the *idea* of sound   clouds   meteors   the sky itself is,
as we are,   porous   permeated   (have you not seen the
light beneath darkness? we rest the oars,   lean out as over
a prow (or is it behind us? into what we know not,   still
our breathing,   douse the cigarette   and listen   to
silence indigenous absence as though a breath beneath
calling sent florets of flame through a membrane still
we listen in anticipation   that is we are still listening

What trumps what?

then write a palindromic (syllable-by-syllable) piece in the shape of a finely wrought iron chair set on a hacienda's patio against the wild heart of a desert sunset, each line ending on the edge of each drome's extent, teetering, just what you'd think. In foreground tiny eyes are waking, little peeps abound, a rustling of anticipation & soft delight. In the mid-ground, an owl straps hisbeak on a dark bough & the moon flashes, almost determinedly, a subtle eighth against the horizon, blond and pale. Man is invisible in this place without extent.

from *Delta Blues*

from *in esse*

Each time he walked in the woods, he could hear the life around him duck for cover. Down by the old plant these were dry sounds. In the pines, soft like laughter after a good joke. When he came to the pond, the syllables were wet and broke on his ear like a watery bell, or a seashell. Entranced, he wrote a score. Once, while conducting his Twentieth, he was lost forever. Birdsong.

A turbo beneath empires of leaf, dark whirlings, abeyance of oblivion welling thru mind of green, existence oozing to skin, galaxies torn asunder, thrown from roof, with sudden emergence of a single word (it's always and only sudden) while this morning upon every surface entire syllabaries are born, then dance in pearly florescence and into the sweet ayre of springe. All my life past telling. Treefrog.

from *in esse*

Perfection is its seed, it sprouts in rose and weed alike, in relations and the dearth of relations, upon the towers of Manhattan, near a mosque in a poor patch of Paris, on a roof in Equador or perhaps it's dreaming just outside the room you are in, dreams you are reading as it enters, or is about to knock and change everything, down to your socks. It's just checking your address, thinking. Delicious word.

Imagine a dense black stone, polished like onyx, set in a universe without stars, possibly without dimension, total dark, eyes torn from mind, streaming black, unending endedness. Now imagine what *it* might be thinking, that there are places language *can't* shine its light, nor fill with its bitterness, nor stroke its tiny balls, the sole flaw of existence is appearance, its redemption without words.

Word at day's end

the onslaught of bronzed grackles begins
with a few scouts in the cypress,
then the cypress flush in its cacophonies
(what music to what ears?) and
the barn dance begins, clouds of grackles from this tree to
that, when one tree flushes the others are
quiet, briefly . . .
tree to
tree on this three acres,
tier over
tier, cross
cut,
looking up,
you could be swallowed . . .
from tree
to tree, finally circling the
bamboo, then a wave flies in
and another, and another, 'til it is
filled, this grove, with the caws, mews, soft
screams, clucking as bass, and the thrashings of
wings
against the stuff of bamboo and other wings, perhaps
torsos, before
they flush again and the earth is silent ex-
cept for someone testing a motorcycle in the distance, but
they are soon back, filling the grove (grackles are
vertical) with epics, sorrows, delights, yet no misgivings,
again
flush,
and again return, this time or the third they
will stay, the thrashing sounds like a water-
fall in a
small cove, walled-in rock, falling four feet,

six across,
bright sound of water splashing, also the feet of

a thousand supplicants at once

in the sand
beneath their chanting
the bright reptilian
mind
which
gradually dies,
calls softer
silence more articulate

title in bold

mind in hold of language, that which casts *us* like dice across time, abyss of page or room's silence, and which throws us as well into each other with such fury, with instruments also the product of language, as we are in a history of words, ancient hatreds singing "Least we never get even" into the street, across mountains and desert, but also cast over stone as a stream glistens, yet would we cross, even to the ankles and knees, would we find the next stone we were sure between each but the current gets suddenly swift and the weather changes as mountains darken and we are caught out in a rush of water up our legs falls certain screaming in mind's dark ear, from slightest slip of phrase to tragedy of sentence in one swift . . . as though we found it there, and as sure

from *in esse*

under weight of words

Like vagina, pure ripe pleasure of pressure (or is it *release*?) wrapped all round him while in his mind, *You vicious cunt!* Tight upbinding swirl of climax, waves on rock, shell impacting shell mid-flight, a baseball bat up back 'a da head, *Great time to snap her neck.* Words smacking of words. Words sodomizing other words. The excavation of witness. Another ontological fix. Words with little penises pissing in your ear, the one you listen with, the one you've forgotten, slipping a stiffy to your memory gland, barking up your fat closet again. Ripe cunt, floppy-eared, red nose of clitoris: The Rodeo of Sex! total slippage of reference. Another night agape in her presence, drifting mid rose-lit testament, words spilling out of words, someday going to be gone long since.

riddle of the abyss

age is telling a long joke, with some apparent joy, early at a party, not all the guests have yet arrived, a first drink freshly in your hand, he's an interesting stranger in no hurry, pausing for laughs, comments, not prolonging the punchline but forgiving it its necessities, standing and laughing and listening, slowly he reaches the part about deepest Pacific blue and the sound of sails at sunset, how their color changes in the changing light, shades of white in encroaching darkness, pewter, you are still young, anything can happen, *yet* is a word you can still use as a soft wedge, argumentation may again be filled with joy, now for witness of sheer mind's leaping, but his words have slowed, slightly, and his head almost turns, then with a light shift in his eye, oh yes, the abyss, I almost forgot

from *in esse*

comma eel

what else is new in the blossoming of wounds, airy fire at every portal, lightning of senses striking you forever dumb, pain as the death of questions, and so on, sweet sweat in all her breath, and all her breathing like mountain air, pines beneath her carcass, while someone's stabbing a cat to death outside the difference between hearing and listening as anticipation blossoms into realization a moment *before* conception (that ripe!, yes, and the red hands, a common field to play on, some mornings dull as a fish, what kind of existence does unrealized sensation have? where does it reside? in a cottage with a thick-ening wife? can she cook? her eyes fill with cataleptic horrors, a cat screams with a human face, we look deep into what remains, as into water, but can find no trace

on the contrary,

death is what makes sense of *every*thing, wrapped in its dream like the soul in a cheap suit, its every thought a landscape only time could prove (or love), what beats in-to your eyes but darkness of fetal sleep, seeps into your nights, how it glistens, the deep shine on oblivion, or in stone blue sky Sunday afternoon late May behind the pond, leaf shadow & sun playing across the page, half shadows, & shadows within shadows & shades, ply over ply of light, shuffling exposures, breeze ruffling trees in succession (and leaves sway), a tractor in the distance, who can say it's not the world at my feet, *too much like thinking to be less than thought* (which doesn't mean it's thinking) so that when it comes it will come sure, clean, & you will be made whole again, as all manner of thing.

from *in esse*

Wet highway before dawn. Last night another room of the dream, a community inside a house, or a few houses, where we all knew each other, we smoked when we wanted, there were women of deep attraction there and a plane without a motor, and later some of us would *go up* at night into a sky so crowded with stars it seemed surface and *idea* of depth, both, and presences leaned out and over us.

He sits like Buddha but leaning hands on knees, he's looking forward and down as though just about to say something, or he is thinking, to *see* what he'll say looking into the thing itself, where what can be said as a mist hovering above it, suddenly clears. He is pausing as he thinks it to himself. There's a snake with its tail in its mouth hanging like a necklace, but going thru his ears, thru his mind.

from *in esse*

It's not what it seems. Summer's the animal given to dream, fat metaphor, given to cast off its cart, without burden of name, no words but its own intractable presence, mind like colors sliding across a floor or if it were more a vertical screen whereon slippages between lucidities extrapolate a universe without machinery beneath, where a bird perches above your door, singing, neither in hope nor despair.

Half way up the mountain there's a gleam you can see for miles. From far below, for instance. You set off to seek it out. It takes years. When at last you find it, over a hard ridge, you find a bottle cradled on a cairn, inside the note: "It's always been thus," by now fully realized, yet you see how this missive can have *its* place as part of the grim joke, the dark machinery of which everyday is more apparent.

from *in esse*

Dawn. You forget where you find the connections, you turn into an empty room & bark instead, the way a building changes in dream, there is nothing to hold what you feel about this which also disappears, & when you look nothing's there, no wife, no children, no houses, no way to hedge a bet, no ironic displacement, maybe you'll lose your anger as well, and all will be the water it is once again.

from *in esse*

late summer

Crowds of clouds each day, thunderstorms every afternoon. Deepening sounds down season's halls resonate in dream. Last night my son tried to stab me in my sleep. Or a man stands on a plateau where small, fat animals are dying. In his mind there was too much of what the intelligence community would call chatter for him to discern any patterns of movement, groupings, messages of mal intent, or sudden losses from stores he thought secure. Lightning in the bowels, black sky tinged with green. Thunder rolls beneath summer's walls, brows at 20,000 feet. Lawn still growing as hair on skull unaware the grand engine has come to a halt and now reverses itself. This time forever. Your last refuge is being torn asunder, nowhere to return, even if you *could* remember.

the museum of sharks

is dark, lit only by candles, each behind a shark, that it might illumine the teeth or shine through the jaw, as though it were milk glass at song's ending. this was supposed to mean something terrible and translucent, the biggest fishing story, or story within the story, Pip's unsettling, sheer mechanism of sea as metaphor for deep dispersal, swirl of loss and accumulation, all manner of matter, thought tucked inside thought, words within words, chapter after chapter spilling out, sheen of sharks' grin on all their latest dreams. what is it to wake just one morning without dying? where a dark window gives back a simple face, clear, limbs know nothing but satisfaction, torso the purest blood running thru it as though torrents of youth might again return as before. who were we? dazed.

from *in esse*

nirvana

libretto of crickets and cars before dawn, Jeri is playing monkey, tearing the house a new one, markets hover on the borders of consciousness full of friendly people wearing wooden shoes and hats, they would fill your pipe, baskets of music and fruit hang with fronds from the rafters, and air drifts slowly down, with light, some-one is playing a joke over the radio, a small group of old men are sharing coffee in what they know will be their last years, laughing, they are blessed, words come with their own illumination, like sharks and hands, hard task-ing of the self even to the edge from which there is no return, & over which no grace descends but that one sets his life to the ripeness of experience, only Gaughin and few others, all islanders, saw it first as fresh paint

incipit

more sea than land, more sky than sea, an alluvial fan of faces spreads across the deltaic plain or rises like smoke into sky, we are subject to its slightest currents, the merest whim of air slicing through air, cloud toppling cloud, the rippling of an eye, untoward word, malicious grin, hint of sneer, such slights to us are the bellowings of gods, what *are* we of which we know so little? the doors to dementia are wide, the way deep and clear, the gallery disappears and men defy all image at single urge, unbounded in boundlessness, he's a syllable, adrift, transubstantiatedfrom languageto language as the mind enters its own silence to ride the black swell, fog each morning, clouds of web cross the road, tree to tree, slung with dew, heavy with moths, fruit is on all the branches

from *Skin*

Proem

portal through which we are seen and whereby we see, as indeed, hands have eyes in the dark and sight at each extent of us, over all our every margin, unwrapped you could fill a room with dust, canvas of sin, cheap costume from props, that with which we wrap the creature (what's crawling around just beneath, your mother? past trapped like hornet under shirt?), or a map to ancient villages filled with laughter, music and dances that will make you spill your drink, the skin has its own climate, winters in its south, where an amphitheater opens onto a harbor, sunset, an old woman telling those gathered that her story will scare them, then going about it slowly, deliberately, and everybody on the last sentence jumping out of their skin.

from *Skin*

all of your skin available to all of mine,

good plan, the skin behind your knees for instance, the pulpy skin around your heart, or by the skin of your eyes, mind's universal petal flowing out, ripe blood & warm nights, a little guitar music, or accordion in the distance, floating beneath moon's scythe long into desert, late bluffs, craters & canyons, villages nested in the foothills, flowing over cities stretched across night's floor, late flight from San Francisco to Dallas as Blaser roared in my ears, his elegiac cadences beneath engines' soft roar, perfect because he took them, steps, again, on the night of his 75th birthday, I saw him smoking outside, and nodded to him his 75th, thinking of his life and the men he had known, floating into their lives, through their skin. Or skin is a fountain, outrush of objects, people, places, memories and speculations, each an echo of its own hollow cave beneath, a throat reminding me of what I always never knew, heart of being there as though released *through* the skin but never passing. It can burn like a liquid shirt of flame, phosphorous, alive to pain they say, or as a cloud, waterfall, birds skimming over its sweet scent after shower, here as presence, that which inhabits the actual, sheaf of life whereon we write.

from *Skin*

floating world

On waves without words, sounding the fat
dead tongue of the sea for what volition makes
of intelligence. I mean, is intention a fuse whereby
we burst or lens thru which we blossom into sight,
mind over all the body? Harbinger of love. The skin
of her eyes tangled in mists, etc., it brings me upon
the long study, and so forth. We are wrappt in flames,
hidden in our own recesses, a commerce unto ourselves!

Oh Angel of Apertures, in dawn's mist golden, hair
streaming before your face, portal to chambers unknown,
of pearl and sleek whiteness grown, protean conduit, alive,
translate me, thus, into thy cortege, and thus the contiguous
universe, realm upon realm of flooding presence, uttermost
permeability, each flowing through each, as light in your
eyes, of motion your belly, form into pure form, I can
almost see through you! slightest beams thru hair limbs
groin piercing forehead in mind's bright swirl, that

I might know what I am, she leads me beside such waters,
depths as still of forest pond, Pergusa, where I fall through and
into the sweet hell within, plain whereon nothing's the same, ever,
never was, but light from each crevice, pore, tremulous, forgiven
as pavement's forgiving, and all that harms the skin is stripped
away at last, as beneath an acid bath, or a blood orgy rippling
through carcass, teeth that capture the soft winged creatures
of each luminous moment and tear them to quaking shreds
the next, aghast, a pollution of eyes, slips from the page . . .

Always naked in someone else's skin, perhaps a "prose *kinema*"
or recognition's first address. *Love starts from form seen*, dances

in mind's light, in sight of such moments, before word's first address, *and takes His place, as subject not object* (turns, returning to remember, as on mirror's surface, in all one's limbs) *in the idea of the possible* (RD), what melody of existence then!, since *Every spiritual form sets in movement the bodies in which (or among which) it finds itself* (EP). That tongue might taste with its mind, spread thinne, sweet light, such actual colors as there are. . . . *Finds* itself! At our skin, empires . . .

That I might see with mine only, delight ignites another rocket over the shimmering terrain of each your every quadrant, caught in fleshed domain, shaking silence with vibrant need, *aroused* we say, brush of blood at margin's surface where we run to drift thru numbed rush then fall back into such quiet as I have ever known, to surface again beyond irony and disrepair and find you there once more at last alive beneath the lucent, quivering depths of temple and storm, silent as the voiceless calm the next morning hovering above a pool in whose face, reflected, stand the massive stone figures of jungle's innermost ruins, limestone, carved, now bathed in shadowy green of triple canopy, scattered like torn organs across the land . . .

A flowing of forms out of forms, then, from the skin, or *in*, screen or scrim on which we read–of soul's origin and aspect (*gaze, look* or *phase*)–where we wear the weather, as leather lair, and with a similar air, mute stare with which rubber wears road, pedal bears to metal, and metal petals salvage-yard, which in turn, turning, wares to rust, or skin as atmosphere, itself placid, enstormed, torn by waterspouts the size of small continents, logged in the South, socked, stuffed, biffed, stuck in, the whole magnificent piano sitting on your chest, torn by blasts where bitter air bares wavering edge of self to pain, no relief, 3rd degree over 90% of his body! where we left him to his long recovery, the tearings and retearings of skin, addictions . . .

Reams of skin to find us in, all our fictions: devastation, recovery, a "new normal," multiple lives of seismic, docile adjustments, redefinitions strewn like indictments over all our mute domain, immortal dust our condition. It holds the body in. Anywhere starts from here, or do we melt on contact with spring's green wings smeared over eyeskin, echoing off canyoned seams deep within, as cortex is skin's infolding, flows into flowers of first morning until all our innermost being is clad in branch, pond, cloud, leaf and sky, color running to the edges of vision, and beyond. The trail starts everywhere from here. Open the door. You're a mirror. The world takes you in.

from *in esse*

one after another, cloud after cloud of voices from the ten-thousand quarters of this evening's land and sky come rising, merging as though married of air, pulsing and falling, sounding their slow drift into silence, listening with their entire beings for response, thus cicadae chant their ancient sibilant wisdom, *Many are with us now*, they sing, raising their voices, *who will never see another spring*

light bounding off earth in autumn, bewildering the gods who were just beginning to tire of their fun, turning from their human games to the feast, on Olympus light exceeds itself, as though bathing every surface, including those long buried, yet the light from this *lowly stage* is of such nature, is of the serious, that even the immortals, gathering the latest sacrifices over their golden tables, are given pause

from *in esse*

words long in coming, he who arrives late at the site of his own singing, and whose continuance is in question, the point of question, silence beneath a single word, the world is gray, nothingness in remission, the trees that bashed their foreheads against the storm, now stand, still in their forms, crickets yet call, azaleas yellow, broken, a bitter tar undercoats birdsong, . . . once again, winter's coming, nothing's done

Rains falling into deeper winter, the air goes sudden white, the fenceline clothes itself in gauze, silhouette of trees, almost somber thoughts in black and white as befits the season, which hides itself in color to trick the soul, errant earth in its wide, drunken arc, spilling itself out, busted teeth across asphalt, who knows how to read? dark syllabaries landing in trees, a spell of crows, branches baring.

from *in esse*

approaching autumn

dead leaves, some the color of cement if cement were rust, scrape my knees on their way to the grave, buried in gravity, the maple still full and maple leaves soft as spring, drops begin their pattern on the pond, leaf rustle hath a new inflection, foliate, smallest sunfish leap, dace shimmer, scurry to every edge where arcs lap, cross, fade back into pond, there is no pause, can be no interruption, below words is sound, beneath sound, silence, then dark cacophonies of need, a river, swells, above sound are the sounds creatures make to each other by which they are known, and above these song, all winding their way into winter, time's valance most acute in the fall, you're over-taken again, nowhere to go but in, listening as babels of rain sweep across the roof of your darkening room

sufferin' succotash

beets meatloaf plenty of Campbell's Soup *Reader's Digest Time Life* television lawn snow watches bikes a dog basketball long distance running Phyllis Platt's legs and smile cars plays birdwatching making radios sweet and sour pussy homework bored senseless in every class the halls of junior high impressive after coming from the suburbs of Detroit with their squat notions of a "physical plant" and then in Bowling Green there were alleys and a mind to explore them the pull of graffiti the slightly lost lobotomized look of those born and raised in same place they are currently living especially if that place is small town America awash in drug stores and Christmas dis-plays yet there are some nights dark & deep as any winter where a man kills his wife or a child tortures a favorite pet

from *in esse*

"God Bless America"

(You'd think they'd at least have the decency to use a comma.) On one of those horrifying morning local talk shows, a woman sits on the couch with oxygen tubes still in her nostrils, "I was intensive care for two weeks," she croaks and begins to cry before I can change the channel. Something has scared the shit out of one of my fellow creatures. The trick is to let the mind adjust *with the eyes* in the dark. Eliminate the figure. Eno was right, all electronic music has allowed us to hear a single note from an acoustic instrument; whereas the sound from a synthesizer results from the movement of a few atoms, only, amplified, notes from a baby grand involve the vibrance of billions. What confusions of being, then, in the human who sounds abeyances of self, or of the world without?

late autumn

There are words like air and water, elemental as iron and heavy breathing. We are on a barrel and the barrel is moving, engaged we say. Or words like driving from the backseat downhill with the accelerator stuck-on-jam in a strange city. The attentions are bamboo, lively green shoots, they stand beneath an olive blue sky, or is it *onion* blue? Has anyone tampered with the controls? No longer at night, the late popping. Here, coffee is of considered significance, as is a good shit. It's autumn. I mean in the fall I never thought would happen. That's a lovely, strange contraption. A car with little legs and a skirt of banana leaves. Baboon umbrella. I need serviced immediately. Mute as planets over my grave, or are they borne on the backs of dolphins, swimming from an antithetical center?

from *in esse*

"Except for what it does to you, death ain't all that bad, especially if you don't mind the smell," he's laughing. It's later. Age's cousin has arrived from another party, some little fanfare, he's well *greezed* already, shiny, making himself obnoxious with that tongue, holding court in the den. He's got his eye on *everything*, he says, glancing up, as though *you'd* understand. You're in the only room.

someone is shouting at night from inside an ice-fishing shed, mid lake, rhythmic and insistent, the great houses mute blotches against bank, merged in tree, barely absences on dim spectral whiteness, in the shed, now a translucent scrim, a single light throws monstrous shapes across walls &, most ominously from within, over a low ceiling, the screaming makes no sense to the observer, yet he wakes to it

from *in esse*

What mind in the wind, dark rain, this road and evening, huddled in the branches, just beginning to starve, the sick, the frail, old, ill and enfeebled all seem to acknowledge it with a precision many may come to know if they're lucky, as they say, in the distant future, pointing somewhere with their brows, somewhere other than here, yet beneath this season's glower, they don't seem so damned sure.

silence, spun of abandonment into thick cords of oblivion, dark roots, amnesia's tentacles, the fibrous hush after caress, absence, and the shuttling thread of everything lost to everyone, including animals, insects: home, heart, purpose; which web, woven, catches you while the tight net of matter relaxes, opens, & you slip thru to such a silence as though you've never known *any*thing ever before

from *in esse*

anvil blows

rain between rains this morning more rain more water on ground, great day for the nightmare of waking once more into your own life, the self you hold in your arms like an unruly child, otherwise *the condition*, of living and leaving at once, like everyone else, what light beneath such darkness? what have you had to accept to be *with* yourself? who *else* do you hold? truly, & so forth, days durable, nights soaked in dream, life leaking through your body, your self wavering in the middle distance or a form that goes before you, always, how will you look in dying? set against what hillside flowering in winter, what reversal in the hard current, four ages of man: love, work, regret, and death, set into the inexorable forward motion of the universe, what luminescence in balance?

there's one season, only,

winter, bare bone on desert floor, not even the memory of meat, and to have lived among juices, what was that? rumor of feathery life long gone since, urge of growth in seed head, languorous exchange of green, cicada as portal to evening's meditation, all buried in fetal sleep, as though they'd never been, sweet descent as consolation, pitch beyond knowing, floor beneath conception, finality without cause, yet one would dream, as bone would wrap itself once more in storied flesh, would *do it over again* only this time without the interference, the bad ass dam breaks, confusions, cataleptic abyss, you can almost see it rise before you, a presence *in the midst*, and straighten, stand, or rotate as a planet, perhaps a reason to have been living all along, but when you reach for it, it's gone.

Death blossoms in oblivion

Each petal, soft as silken purse to thumb, returns the luster of darkness beneath hammered gold, the stare in eye, each whispers your nearest name, and is then silent. Cars and trucks round the curve into deepest winter's night (I woke wondering what is it, that rush I heard, the wind! What does my father hear just this side of that which opens to exclude him? Scorpioidal cyme, the *whole inflorescence* curved on itself, like space, both there and not there, where he sits beneath its pitch of sheer, takes nothing in. Shims between a golden door and the unfurling of oblivion. Or takes in every blessed thing, his face a screen, reflection, an empty basket. Death shuffles the deck again and again. He never seems to tire of his stupid joke. Has all the living globe as audience, attentive.

free rain

would we have an alphabet of flowers and flames, notion of sheer as falls off falcon's wing, stoop's onrush of air that paralyzes prey, wall-shattering distances in middle ear, letters forged like leaves on autumn's air, blistering with color, acidic light bleaching the sky more each day with advent of winter, deepest night, drained of all but stars, haunted by Orion, a bewilderment of constellations inhabits each stroke, in the wrist of every eye a graven image, script in which each word's a wave cast into a world of waves, leaves ticking in the cold, wide night air of the actual, where all else matters, punctuation like ships rocking in their berths mid-storm or a horse in its stall as flames fall upon upwending horsy screams, just for the shining in our brain, wonder of coldest predawn

from *in esse*

burial of caves

Saint-Saëns saw a sea in his sleep. Dropped in a key. Since he'd visited a zoo only that day (trying to win the favors of one slight puff some thirty years his junior), his dream threw up the stuff of tigers, a twirling crock, one bird's full throated, *Barely dying yet, boss*, crest stiff in morning's rigor of the quick (she stirs?) music is always right in middle of (definitely indefinite), where surface turns, blinks, swirls with what's moving to edges (likewise indefinite), always (if listening).That is, sweet caves she had & all her caves gave way to caverns, each a life renewed, a *site* in which to bathe existence in the waters of her oblivion. Saint-Saëns forgot all about the animals, & his music disappeared into night sky, into ranges of her hair, the soft light of her eyes, & into all her tangled being.

from *in esse*

"And in the end there's no end but forgetting"

–Mayer

begins shredding plans, then desire to plan. future gone, it devours past. memories dim in shade, darkening, cast a burnished sheen against the pit, and then are gone, as though they'd never been. saves present for last, all but the very moment on which you float, a circular plain billowy period on its back, thank god you fit. it's infinite. there's not even water below. no distance. like slowly erasing yourself til you disappear or discover a pattern beneath the scribblings of what's-going-on-right-now. but everyone's someone else again and all you got left are your obsessions and the pain. yellow of parrot's beak. woman's claw. animals in her neck. running savanna of flesh. what's she sitting on is *gone*. you continue. 'til you don't. what hole at the end of descent? what whiteness?

no wiser and worse for the wear

the possible leans in a doorway,
his back to you,

you are in a chair,
in the room,

beyond the silhouette of his form,
plains shimmer in a hard summer day,

the room sounds like just after loud music,
he shifts his head, a shoulder,

you are trying to draw his face
from memory,

he whistles,
you take another drink

paragraphs like the bending of grasses
in a soft wind,
going from one thing
to another,
the conversation of two old friends
the first night, not having
seen each other
for years

Solstice Two Days Out

C r i s t o s
r e t u r n t h y
m e a s u r e
s u n n e s
s o u t h w a r d
j o u r n e y s
s p e n t s t i l l
t h i s d o w n w a r d
p u l s e m e n d
t h y e a r t h
a g a i n
s t i t c h i t
w i t h s w e e t
f l o w e r s

C r i s t o s
r e t u r n s h i n e
f o r t h s t i l l t h y
d o w n w a r d c o u r s e
m o n t h s
d e a d
c o l d
s t e m
f r o z e n
r e n e w t h y p r e s e n c e
b r i n g w a r m t h
s u n n e t o b e a r o n
a l l t h y l i v i n g e a r t h

Word at morning

bronze grackles   &   blackbirds
in their unsettling   before dawn   in the bamboo grove
to which
I have come   (in mine)   to sound

in their sound   dark cacophonies   conjunction of
creature in
creature need   wide mewing, clucking, crying   and
clicking   that rattle   in the predawn   echo
of
their splashing
off opposing tangle of
life / lives
then a brief diminution   as clusters rise
into the upper reaches of two pear trees which have been swallowed by
the bamboo   lost in their attentions
then as loudly as before
such pulsing   two or
three times   before
a deep, sudden hush
(like a dead man catching his breath)
and the first string   peels out
west
goddamned beautiful fucking
tube, wavering,   stretching   for
miles   anywhere from four
to over twenty individuals   deep   as they exit
sometimes in clouds   thicker tubes   pulsing

then I saw
a hawk   not fifteen yards distant   at
my height   patrolling the coulee

surely with so much life there must be
glorious accidents galore

light in all the branches

he flies back and forth every few minutes
finally the tube is pinched off inexplicably
surely like a good shit
I hear thousands more yet in the grove
their music rises
splashes over light, pink on verge of orange
mere yellow
leaking into the east

Dawn Patrol
flies back
and forth
once more

then they hush again and a thick pulsing cloud comes out
pulling another tube even thicker than the first
more miles of birds scat into distance
and while I'm reading their wavering script it runs backward
like spokes of film as language in dream
then
a tube to the north also headed west from the grove
behind the carport now flows into the first and I
am surrounded in birds' near circle woven
script in motion glowing
just like on televison trying to read
blest? or cursed?
could I tell the difference?

hawk sits in his tree

to remain throughout

oblivion spun of absence into a fine liquid strand, deepest purple, almost black, poured into an opening at the top of your skull, you of course are transparent, shivering as the thread plunges into your cranium, also of liquid, translucent, a dream's definition of *stealth*, widens as it slows, then the slightest feathers of purple slide from the strand, unfurl to permeate your every crevice, impossible that the body should bear, the weight of it! absence grounded in the actual, brute stare, even your saliva stinks of it, a little hand caresses your nuts as you feel *an exploratory finger*, that is, you'll go on missing them forever, a gray word like cement into the soft velvet glove of predawn as westward grackles fly, also into such weather, dark calculus of being, what's not going away

from *Stormy Mondays*

If it didn't exist I wouldn't believe it myself

driving in each morning through man's haphazard arrangements land strewn with houses sheds vehicles wires poles signs buildings standing and falling apart pocketed in the drear light of late february early march, the clatter of creatures in their cars trucks & trailers, codes of public traffic, fetal sleep, all prime pissing steroids, livers grinding to keep up, hearts the dying of horses in this fragile fuselage the chest, so we're going to market are we? delivery vans flatbeds roads streaming over roads, now we're getting someplace, they're screaming in cabs lost beneath glass gasping and grasping at the wheel, all that cement and nowhere to go, the land of their lives forgot under considered over subscribed or just plain fucked.

eye in memory's socket

is cliff, to remember, falling off last
night in dream, the argument allusive, possibly
insane, you suspect before catching yourself
"at it again," a woman's face, for instance,
coining summer morning and trees, not to mention
the ecstatic, a dilation in the melody of small town
in utero, Bowling Green, even Perrysburg was
alien, rubbing shoulders with a shitty, little
city for all there was of it, and for what there
wasn't . . .? what? lives in abeyance otherwise
without coordinate life, ordinal song, deep hymn
of gravity, pulling us along (if you look at it
straight), mind in eye's socket, touching light &
all it sings of the body, flailing, falling off

from *Heart*

Proem

of center the core, eighty-first flower, blossom adrift beneath aortic arch on mind's floor, floating in oblivions of body, feeds on itself, ripe pig, oft made meagre, hard, a ball of snot, shit wad, or in its soundings, recognitions clear (blood of such thought!), harbor, suspension of laws in sudden seizure, seat of affections, point equidistant from all peripheries, of source the definite (*at last!*) from which it may be said, *The universe goes only outward from here*, how you might know where you are, to what bounds, repository of emotions, reservoir, cistern, where you go when you would learn, be certain, one man making the world as best he can, even as others do otherwise, it's easy to be an idealist, especially if you don't have to mind the evidence, what I come to do is hard

from *Heart*

the country I come from

cast of broken teeth on an endless plain river
ditch road bank trail wood corn & asphalt mansions
of a million rooms in each upending shard ice wall re-
freezing in the contending floe after storm rooms
like caverns of skulls over limb-littered plains after battles
lost like the bones of ice grew eyes and we its mind all
along the Maumee where it rained and froze the branches
snapped swamp roots pricked from muck where great
snappers and quarries of small mouth carp and maybe
Jimmy Hoffa caught deep in their waters preserving what
is best left forgotten like a life without any reason other
than the maintenance of self-insistence in a land where
water-towers mutely grope the sky a vein-blue haze in
every distance due to the slow decomposition of time

from *god, metal, planet, plant*

Canticle of Recovery: Burn Ward

Beneath leaves floating on water, *in*
water, over stones round as heaven is
round, and hell square, to set against
it, orb as platform of stars, on earth,
here, *there are no straight lines in nature*,
where I, flowing amid the float of leaves
in wind and wave and water, suspended over
river stone, lost in ten-thousand shades
of green and brown, beneath sky's icy blue
egg, and midway on my journey, wake
between this world and that, from which,
riding the slightest of breezes, angelic
voices, a chorus in swift approach, dis-
mount and comb my hair; and on sister
currents, equally restorative, attendant
graces advance through nature's several
portals, each to an apportioned sense as
though conceived and born simultaneously,
proportionate to their occasion, wherewith
all pain is washed in heaven's deepest, lost
abyss, amnesia laving the cusp of every tender
curve and conduit as though fingers, lips
and eyes with tiny hands might sprindge such
balm as that which over-spreads skin's every
surface, whereon oblivion casts its silent,
shining net across all the tortured terrains
of my being, at last!, reticulations within reticulations
(flowing on, sleep without pain . . .

. . .

when out of dark
arched head vertical eye & fangs black fever of adder-
infested dream whiplash coil and snap of spine in
crack of paroxysm . . . freakwire a black swan shot from
sky mars maddened flukes swimming in sun-glare
the size of elephants of whales mammoth widening flange
of pain spreading across sky slipping from senses all over
again loss of reason's purpose fiery dog
licks marrow with mean mug and brightening glare
teeth talon tongue each a worm torn from night's core a burning
brand hissing my name tosst sinks in eye-
ball cortex all my mental flesh lonely sorrow amid
columns burnished by dark flames they have torn
me apart the angels and have scattered me
to coincidence and back whereto they bind me
that I might serve as definition of *horrific death*
else pain is simply a toy for them that we might bounce
and twist and heave beneath the hysterical sky all broad day
rivers tying themselves in knots eye of viper beneath desert
coiled and cleft chipped from cliff amid the tumbling of
shadows such scratchings as meaning's way torn from
inmost lobe heart in mind crazed on
a spit turning the crackling of my own juices in my
ears . . .
yet late . . .

In tall grass a small hen sings:

Leafy care, my darlings,
for the oil on thy wings,
that thou'dst avoid all lime
and fowler's snare, rocks
of boys who know no harm,
also shun lantern and wave,

but follow sunne in its decline
  that thou may'st southward
sing of that which here you
  find, and thus remember tree
and glen, the morning shine
  on valley's bough, leaf and
web, the singing in thine head
  when first thy hunger was
appeased, and looking out upon
  the world with wonder, saw
love, and caught at thy breath.

Love hath reason, reason none.

Longing bringeth peace.

Deeper the peace, more lofty
  the desire, thus clouds in
concert as they drift, fluorescent
  tipped, arrayed on evening's

canvas, splayed in colors
  of soft regret, ballasted in
blackness, yet hot with day,
  haunted by light, sing,

more lofty the desire, keener the
  satisfaction, mind saturated
with senses, informed by intellect,
  grounded in body, and so forth;

consider the ant, lit in our
  reflection, its shadow's cast

east to west, toward sun in fast
decline beneath the rim as if in

half appeal, Nothing of this body's
amorphous bounty, wrapped
in light, can be concluded but
by thought of night wherein

we blossom beyond vision yet
within sight sounding heaven's
vault for what remains of love
after day in daylight's spent.

Love hath reason, reason none.

All love is born of mountains, mountains
sing, *though valleys, plains, and oceans claim*
as much, we have the better suit, for among us
can be found certain reason to be airborne

yet welded to the ground as we look out and
over . . . , what climbing of trees can match
this swirl?, the vertigo of existence, living
in the blast of such moment as this is to

intuit scale: bird, cloud, mountain, and thus
to what's beyond, eternal night beneath sky,
and realize just how *large* we are. . . , *is this not*
love?, the measure of our kind, to look and find

nothing wanting, beyond contention, nor true, nor
false, but as the pulsing of stars, the weight of
each in time's reticulations, shimmering wave

across the emptiness of which we are a part.

Love hath reason, reason none.

then crash
landing onto a planet miasma of pain coating
the surface to a depth of 50,000 meters
no mountains
no hills just
one vast stinking sinkhole burning sludge
utter melt of all defenses
in the first nano-moment
planet as writhing hell
septic stew of self aflame
sinking . . .
in body's sewer
heart of pain
and more pain pain without name
pain cavity as identity
sinking without remission
whittled to the infinite not
even a shaving in the supernovaen
swirl cosmic blossoming
mars black at the center
of fire bottomless

pain

pain beneath that

where moments are decades . . .

Dawn sits on the rim. Gone the hours of waiting, merest light
To wan, in which he could see the fingers of one hand, finally,
Darkness glistening with anticipation as night loped slowly on, gave

Over to the vast diurnal urge, everything turning *toward*, if only
To the future, light splashing up and over and into all the
World, both constant *and* immediate, while ever presence
Strings melodic line through branch and vine, ribbons of birdcall
Weaving thru hedgerow, leaf and pine, swinging on attention's
Brachiation, throbbing in treeline, as heart in orange robes pours over
And fully forth, as though purpose were discernable at last . . .
A dream in the death of dying, also threaded, beyond design.

Of morning is such melody, in earliest hours unconstrained,
Ripeness of sight and sound, affections flung skyward to airs
Divine, music never heard by mortal ear, nor aspect seen by eye,
But in light of likeness, cloud clambering over cloud, bounded-
Lessness over the bound, beyond reason, thru chambers of deep
Intent, a dilation, to be up and doing, immediate branch held
Forth in future death, sways back, flows ever toward version's first
Address: the coming and going at once, bulge of all things beyond
The extant, host saturated with the infinite, a conduit in every sense *through*
Which whatever may sustain us might expeditiously advance, aware
Such salvation surrounds us that we might in becoming *be*, as of many,

One, the same as one is, or may be, indefinitely finite (*that* precise).
That is, the sun rose in him and he–variously cut, exoskeleton
Torn by acetylene, crackled back, lens seared at seam, slashed
Sack, node of *pains unutterable* (yet all too apprehensible), giving
New distinction to the endurance of horrific seconds in succession,
Anticipation only of ever-demanding insistence–from hell returned to
Life, newly awake in light of consciousness and *its* orders, digit scoring
The wall, directive tagged to brick, refuse stitching streets with sign,
God spore no longer the insane scrabble tangled in *what is*, but a *voice*,
So that he, battered and torn, to witness borne, bound, burnt offering,
Woke to what brought him there, to that mattress, pain dissipating

In dawn's raw air and lassitude of hospital bustle, *the solely singular*,
Mute glory for the miming of gods, meat steaming in sun's radiance,

Black mount behind, projected on wall, a shade, a small hole dilating,
  Within it a pulsing orange dome, as the blade of mind seared *its*
Imperative into the frontal lobe of day, the edge of what he *must*, honed
  By light, drop forged in moment's clamor, actually *do*. So, . . . twice
Damned, entombed by stone, hounded by words, streets and visions,
  Torn by flame, buried in coma, pain, remission only in forgotten oblivions,
Yet always more pain, until tortured by withdrawals' emptiness, blasted ox
  Or oak, zapped from above, behind, articulate as a burning torso,
He was struck sure, certain as blade or brain, knowing the pattern plain,

When down his cheeks two runnels, flowing in first light, glowed,
And on his pillow two globes, growing, set forth a subtle rose.

sic transit

Never too much merriment.
–Spinoza

Moon hovers alive high in the south
before dawn sky nearly washed of stars yet
Mars dances a delicate moth
flutters just west as Moon's craters canyons
chasms and cliffs saturated
with light
bounce on the fat glass
bulb of eye
it's 5:15 a.m.

. . .

four hours later a crop duster unseen in
the distance weaves thru mowers near
and far cars on the curve
cicadae and crickets
calling
birdsong risen
now falling woven with duster's drone a parabolic
arc that buries its head in the earth then turns
to grind the air to mush again and again
sounding its
integration with time

. . .

a yellow butterfly scouts
the front yard its map
articulate as the duster's
dancing sheen stitching greens

and browns and grays
on a fiery
point of light
residual glow in mind
hours after

. . .

afternoon's vast canopy
stretched into evening as
massive clouds roll in from the west
arching over all things (how many silos
in a single cumulonimbus? banana spiders hang
head-downward as an emblem of patience nets
dusted in late summer's pollen slightly
greenish bronze
if seen from the side
distant thunder and lightning . . .

. . .

What is it to commend your spirit to such orders?

from *Clouds*

Were I on *top of the world* these clouds would
hang above me still, such their towering laughter,
ancient Spanish dragon flowing into pocked profile
of crone, dark harmonies suspended in the abyss,
arrive to stand the morning sun, a wake, depth
of canyon, rivers of sight in streaming rifts and
corrugated rills, califs and camels, or what man
will, then, of love, sky's vocabulary, pleas nested
in vowels, wisdom of cumulus beneath a cirrus
sibilance (telling us . . . what?, that we are not
alone?, or that we are, must find each other in
ourselves, all things passing through all things,
memory's radiant vasculature, a sign, *the way
is never fixed*, falling down long avenues . . .

from *Clouds*

Seaside Sunlight Summertime Suicide Vomit

gulls call gull calls beneath walls of
cloud upward tending blent light
over the furniture of heaven but his shoes
are missing and a blackberry stain surrounds his penis
the wine of mistake misunderstanding mystery
swirl maybe he's not even dead the cave they found
him in day the fish were ferocious spitting out hooks
to get at the men before the sky went crazy etc.
windows high in eye's study dark splotch beside the
head when we got there the crabs had been at him
half a day but they steered completely clear
of the small pond of vomit odd
I thought and couldn't get shut of it haunting
all my daylight hours I take pills not to remember
what happens at night view of bay from there enough
for dozens of suicides like someone got
their claw stuck and the mechanism took it
off clean at the grinding howls you can
almost hear (in vision is such sounding
and then
the clouds tend upward to strange
aspect climb the sky to crouch
as though the lesser demons have gained the upper
hand again and all hell's on its head
pouring out danger itself on fire
fed on avarice, envy, malice, blind
fucking spitting hatred, twisted needle,
drowning in consumption diplomats lawyers
politicians and all their concubines or that
might be just me a tin shield two years from

retirement with a gun I've never had to
use even as a threat name's Max
used to be a woos but toughened up got it?
now age and weariness distemper the heart sheer
screeching boredom tier over tier little did I know
however that *this* was to be the case that would end all that
the smooth slide into oblivion soft and slow
with a cup of joe a fresh paper and a pack a' smokes
no this case turned that inside out
frazzled my dispensations spewed its toxic mash over
all the rest of my life damn thus the language of clouds
beyond cave mouth *locus delicti* with tremolo sinistro
nearly audible beneath the crooked lap of waves
on cave wall and the open suck of massive space
beyond the dirty little harbor town ubiquitous
beached whale driven mad smothered by
its own mass on our shingles shits to our
poverty the can filled with drunks
and sodomites fornicators with beasts wife
beaters and man haters in whose
confusions we call the communal to
witness "is it not thus and
so ?" bearing our lives to sea or plant each
morning to be caught and canned
with the rest of the fish in-
discriminate then borne on wheels and
rails to feed pets of the nation had
I known then what now I know I
might have thrown my badge into that pond of
vomit watching it dissolve in the acids move to
a strange city and bag groceries for the rest
of my days finding what pleasure pleasure
affords and sleep
maybe not
for what I found of the alien in kind

dreaming the solution I mean
if a black and white crime scene photograph can
be shot in livid technicolor (and it can)
then come alive in three dimensions
such dreams the thickness of all
sides the corpse getting to sit up
and smoke but I have to lend him one of mine so's not
to mess with the evidence he nods knowingly
seeing it's a Camel® scratched into life with
a crack from an original Zippo® the cave walls also
thick and furry of sizable extent now in the black and white
of electron microscopy beneath strobe of wraith-light
wherein the puddle of vomit glowed as though
the negative of a colored movie being caught
out in the Rockies but metallic golden
mercury sheen to flowing platinum another
universe in each liquid roll and ball
of metal I thought as I leaned
over a story un-
folds another death and another
each a flash in wavering crystal glare of loss and
recovery one after another dying head shots
fluttering into the depths of the pond
that I was led to believe he had coughed up
and given me indelibly if only in such dream
guilt to bear caustic stain of life
without remission where even my greatest pleasures
which rose on the plain towering magnificent above
the domestic skyline of daily habits to prick
the sense of stars themselves as they are now
dust in my mouth
all else follows . . .

Whatever Thing Death Be

pillow of desiccated flies as an emblem of silence, echo-less echoes of shadows tangled in shadings gone down long halls of dreamer-less dreams, streets and visions in a language of clouds, lost beyond floundering, or mind's certain peace wherein the walls of all its senses fall back and out, as though waking from a fevered dream, clear and weak, smelling, but a shower and breakfast will begin to fix all that, life stripped of itself like the past and a morning so lightly sweet it could crack your nut, shifting grammars of oblivion in mind's peace, a mass of vowels, liturgy of silent, imageless words slipping in sky's syntax until friction itself, with purchase, directive, resolve, and even goal disappears in imagination's figment, all things passing thru all things, what of its manner might be known

abeyance of nothingness

wisp across surface of the nonextant, birth
glow, stitching light of sunrise with sunset's
rose caught in the unfolding penumbral scroll,
from before the beginning, into a fabric of deep
space, save for when that massive orb rolls, me-
chanical and silent, across oblivion, swallowing
sky itself in its display, or a bumbling rush of gnats
just before dusk, late autumn, weave their cursive
pheromonic trails with frenetic insistence on whatever
might become, over shine's abyss, of them and us,
or simply the complexities of each moment crashing
into the complexities of the next, replete with clatter,
a roomful of waiters, say, mowed down by silencers,
a comedy of dishes and trays, silver and glassware, *quelle*
surprise!, or flatly, as a table pitches into life, riles mule-
like, as love might, into a time that death, apparently,
has forgotten, as life in its season, brief as a day, an hour

"the absolute has no price"

–Bowles

An old man sits in his chair, exhausted. What
he had been no longer exists, nor can he remember
what it was, his life, yet he is still here, weak
and confused, at times scared. Outside, the wind
howls. It rains. It snows. Hours. He sees nothing
of the storm, nor later of the light that reaches
beneath clouds, from beyond the mountains, to
twist in the broken web of branches, glittering,
nor the play of water on water, the hardness
of night air, how it swallows everything. Never
again will he see such beauty as once was pleasure
to him. Now the world is merely a place to be
gone through, simply, meanly, with suffering. No
answer is sufficient for this, none is required.

Lost lake

where my dad and I once paddled up upon a bull
moose in the fading light standing a few feet from
shore, not lifting our paddles, turning them sideways
on the upstroke to slice silently as fog we slipped
in and when we were thirty feet away, or so memory
has it, the enormous bull lifted his head, beard dripping
wet marsh grass, a flowing of waters that seemed to defy
the fading light, luminescent, colorful, *a god!* I thought
to myself. One night when my father was dying of congestive
heart failure and Altzheimer's, calling for help repeatedly,
though I was right there, but also hitting pockets of lucidity,
I reminded him of the moose, how his raised head shadowed
sky's weak light as he looked at us, before slowly turning,
as though we barely existed, and walked back onto an island
or finger of land, beard dripping, as an artist's brush might drip
in lost light, and I asked my father if he remembered the
moose, and he had, complete with the part about a god.

Floral Risers

–Dad

steps at spring's banquet, headful onto
summer's dias, commence then long
advance beyond beginning's slumber
                                        (wakenings upon wakenings . . .
                                                  flowers upon flowers . . .
      in anticipation, sky's lost blue in stuttering
      darkness, negative beneath eye's light where
      mind wonders, coldly, Is this all? Was there never
      only always cause, origins stripped like petals
of a lily who would counsel clouds to rain, that earth
be brought to its fulfillment, dawn not lost in desolation's
day? This same white valley claims a recognition
of mortality might delicately shade our eyes amid
the blare and jostle of an actual street.
                                                        A memorable fancy–
   How angels filled the sky adrift or falling or
   streaming outward to morning's clarion
   flare–wherefrom a spirit, thus aroused, called
   out, etc., All is accomplished where I go
   forth, Horses of the charnel house swim leagues
   through dream into abattoirs of light. They are
                  of the gods (and so forth). The lively apple. The willsome
                  nut. Or storm risers on the heels of avarice, rapacious
                  greed, penury of spirit, even irony wears its face, thus
                  leeches thru boundaries, soaking gardens to suck dry
                  the roots of muthos, entire academies addressed to
                  degradation of self and self's deep share, to light's
                  occlusion, and to error . . .

         in the face of which

                                                        only flowers

(dawn just now!

a melody strung from spring's *potentia*, living at our furthest edge
–in air just the other side of skin–
thence urged into summer through sweet flesh, to core, and lower, taproot
boring earth, chthonic pull head downward in fullness search
brought upward forth and into fruit the which
in autumn is termed *purpose*
if only
that the song be once again renewed after
a meditative interlude (or where it is harsh, such soft steps of several color cross
field newly green awake in lavender light beneath sky
of ciel, etc., shall give us certain cause that we rejoice
at end of such a winter sweet stakes in all death's heart

Notes

21 "more furious self" (an angel), variant, Stevens.

22 "Civil rights for / white folk," David Duke, Republican candidate for governor of Louisiana in 1991 and former member of the KKK.

"Miracles of the Virgin in Tickfaw, La." (sightings of the Virgin in the sun over a field outside Tickfaw), newspaper 1989.

"Build me a small fire" (so he might fry in his own fat while yet alive), Southern folktale.

27 "a spinning and bursting of the sun" (sightings of Virgin Mary), newspaper.

28 "her small feet on the alter steps" (Mary, age three, dancing on the temple steps), "Infancy Gospel of James" (*Protevangelium Jacobi*), Christian Apocrypha.

"Χαιρέ!" (Chaire). Trans. "rejoice," "be glad," or more commonly, "hail." Often accompanies approach of goddess or Mary.

32 "the world stopped," "the word stuck," "birds still," "in cave mouth," "light leaps" (birth of Christ) "Book of James, Or *Protevangelium*," Christian Apocrypha.

39 "Dearest! You're the one love of my life. There has never been / another. Not really" from letter, W.C. Williams to Flossie while hospitalized for severe depression after a stroke.

Ftnt.: Historical records included in New England Genealogical Society's book on the Proute line which led to my paternal grandmother.

40 "Dearest. Even / with others, I only thought of you. Please believe me," from letter, W.C. Williams to Flossie as above.

43 "*willingness of heart*" (basic American characteristic), Fitzgerald.

"*hora prima*," first hour of Roman day.

"Sweetest stand of timber! All the way to Mexico!" Kirk Douglas.

"Structure of remembering what is not a dream," Mayer.

"teeth in the calf / of his wife," from a biography of Walter Anderson, artist.

"*up to the eye and soul*" (fully charged), Olson.

46 "the relaxation and dilatation . . ," from definition of "diastole," *American Heritage Dictionary.*

47 Illustration. Drawn by Tammy Charron from a picture of a lintel leading to a room in which the actions depicted occur: a vision serpent rises like smoke from the burning blood-soaked cloth in the basket (bottom center). From the serpent's jaws the presence of the initial ancestor, "the founder," comes forth to give the supplicant instructions, in this case apparently rather pointed. The glyphs are reversed, meant to be read, scholars speculate, from within, through the rock. See Linda Schele and David Freidel, *A Feast of Kings: The Untold Story of the Ancient Maya* (New York: Morrow, 1990):266-68.

49 "No narrative / is natural, a discourse, not a series / of events," variant of Todorov.

"a sense / of proportion plugged into an unmeasurable" & "the transformation concepts /undergo before magical discourse is possible," Gerald Burns.

51 "*the steadiness / of its shining*" (condition into which the existent emerges), Heidegger.

"*state of / permanent decision*" (consciousness), Heidegger.

52 "*limns* that / limit [one]," Olson.

"what any of us are / inside of" (limits), Olson.

"*conjectural hypothesis / comparable to the existence of invisible light?*" (the self), Stephen E. Toumlin, "Self Knowledge and the Knowledge of the Self," *The Self: Psychological and Philosophical Issues*, ed. Theodore Mischel (Totowa: Rowman, 1977): 291-317.

"new complexities within / relationships long familiar," variant, Toumlin, ibid.

53 " Life fluent even in wintriest / bronze," Stevens.

A"*piece of petalled / and delicate utility*" (the body), Stephen Ellis.

"*Nullam obicem ponere.*" Trans. "Let nothing obstruct," Middle Ages, said prior to prayer.

54 "kenosis," emptying onself in preparation to follow God's intention. When applied to Christ, kenosis theology is discredited by the Catholic Church.

"*That which exists through itself . . . / is what is called meaning*," Olson.

"Experience of something that remains and is / constant" (art), Duncan.

"*Rills to suggest flickering / movement*" from Dore Ashton, "A Straggler's View of Gorky," *Arshile Gorky: The Breakthrough Years* (exhibition catalogue): 55.

"I come from 36 / Union Square," de Kooning's answer to a query as to whether he influenced Gorki or vice versa. (Gorky's studio had been at 36 Union Square.)

55 "*Everything / is accomplished through the senses,*" *The Horn Island Logs of Walter Anderson.*

"*resemblance and dis- / resemblance*" (basis of rhyme/awareness), Duncan.

"*Of rhythm is image*," Olson.

56 "*Relaxation and dilatation . . . ,*" definition of "diastole," *American Heritage Dictionary*

"*Lights the openness of the region into / which it comes*" (the emergent as it comes into existence), Heidegger.

"*with the whole galaxy blowing up just to say something*," slight variant of Spicer.

62 "*high / substance*" (poetry), Stephen Ellis.

"The Apennines," moon's largest visible mountain range (named after the range in Italy).

"*and men who will only find / them there*," continuation of Creeley's epigraph.

"How is it far if you can think it?" Confucius, tr. Pound.

63 "*solidity most spatial in its intent / against the drifts and appearances that rise / and fall away in time*" (the emergent work of art), Duncan.

"*Never more than / at this moment*" (paradise), Olson.

64 The narrative of "The Boat" (33-34) continued.

"And out, onto the smoking / bank," variant of Ginsberg.

75 "*sic transit gloria mundi*," trans. "Thus passes the glory of the world," an incantation originally recited along the procession during papal coronation ceremonies but later used secularly as an elegiac phrase.

Earthlight, like earthshine, refers to the light reflected from earth onto a new moon.

"*Surely thou shall not die*," variant, Satan to Eve in Genesis and Milton.

"life / is preoccupation with itself," Olson.

79 "*Those rayes which all these flames / doe nourish*," Daniel.

81 "*absolute structure of desire*" (clouds), Mayer.

"*the 'not yet' diminishes as / the concealing shadow disappears*" (emergent form), Heidegger.

89 "*the infinite rising / and passing away which itself neither rises or passes*," modification of Hegel's "Appearance is the rising and passing away that does not itself pass away, but is 'in itself,' and constitutes the actuality and movement of the life of truth."

90 "*the way goeth, or leadeth hither, or / thither*" (the misdirection of "metaphor, tropes and other rhetorical figures instead of words proper"), Hobbes.

"*Whereas ways cannot go nor proverbs speak*," Hobbes.

92 "*For by death has been wrought / greater change / than hath been shown*," slight variant of Bierce.

94 "*All things shall be accomplished / through the senses*," from *The Horn Island Logs of Walter Anderson*.

95 As "Our crossing was a shadow" (64) was a continuation of "The Boat" (33-34), this "completes" "*sic transit*" (81).

100 "Deep / Wanderers," planets traversing the zodiac, classical metaphor.

106 "*the closest twin to / life there is*" (art), Olson.

113 "*And the power to tell is glory*," Creeley.

115 "*nec mortale sonans*," trans. "of no mortal sound."

117 The "experimental inspection of the hitherto unknown," Gorki.

120 "now that / the relative has been restored to include . . . ," from Olson's "now that the relative has been restored to include the Absolute."

131 "*in accordance with the tendency to falling essential / to everydayness*," (inability to form a viable notion of death), variant from Heidegger.

"*pearly spouse*" (Christ seen in a vison), Edward Taylor.

132 "*nil admirari*," trans. "by nothing astonished."

"*increasingly / hardened forgetfulness of being*" (negligence of existence), Heidegger.

137 "*in esse*," trans. "in actuality," "having actual existence."

143 "*too much like / thinking to be less than thought*" (processes of the world, leaf scuttle, etc.), Stevens.

151 "prose *kinema*," Pound.

"*Love starts from form seen, . . . / and takes His place, as subject not object . . . / in the idea / of the possible*," Duncan.
152 "*Every spiritual / form sets in movement the bodies in which (or among which) it finds / itself*," Pound.
177 "*there are no straight lines in nature*," Cezanne.
179 "*Love hath reason, reason none*," Shakespeare.
182 "*solely singular*," Shakespeare.

Available from

UNO PRESS

General Titles

**The Not Yet* by Moira Crone, 978-1-60801-072-1 (2012)

A Baltic Anthology Book 1: Contemporary Latvian Poetry, edited by Inara Cedrins, 978-1-60801-050-9 (2012)

A Baltic Anthology Book 2: Contemporary Estonian Poetry, edited by Inara Cedrins, 978-1-60801-052-3 (2012)

A Baltic Anthology Book 3: Contemporary Lithuanian Poetry, edited by Inara Cedrins, 978-1-60801-051-6 (2012)

**The Astral Plane: Stories of Cuba, the Southwest and Beyond* by Teresa Dovalpage, 978-1-60801-078-3 (2012)

**The Man Who Wanted to Buy a Heart* by Leonard S. Bernstein, 978-1-60801-073-8 (2012)

Post-Katrina Brazucas: Brazilian Immigrants in New Orleans by Annie McNeill Gibson, 978-1-60801-070-7 (2011)

New Orleans: The Underground Guide (2nd Edition) by Michael Patrick Welch & Alison Fensterstock, 978-1-60801-079-0 (2011)

The Saratoga Collection, edited by Terrence Sanders, 978-1-60801-061-5 (2011)

**The Garden Path: The Miseducation of a City*, by Andre Perry, 978-1-60801-048-6 (2011)

Before (During) After: Louisiana Photographers Visual Reactions to Hurricane Katrina, edited by Elizabeth Kleinveld, 978-1-60801-023-3 (2010)

**Beyond the Islands* by Alicia Yánez Cossío, translated by Amalia Gladhart, 978-1-60801-043-1 (2010)

**The Fox's Window* by Naoko Awa, translated by Toshiya Kamei,978-1-60801-006-6 (2010)

Black Santa by Jamie Bernstein, 978-1-60801-022-6 (2010)

Dream-crowned (Traumgekrönt) by Rainer Maria Rilke, translated by Lorne Mook, 978-1-60801-041-7 (2010)

**Voices Rising II: More Stories from the Katrina Narrative Project* edited by Rebeca Antoine, 978-0-9706190-8-2 (2010)

**Rowing to Sweden: Essays on Faith, Love, Politics, and Movies* by Fredrick Barton, 978-1-60801-001-1 (2010)

Dogs in My Life: The New Orleans Photographs by John Tibule Mendes, 978-1-60801-005-9 (2010)

New Orleans: The Underground Guide by Michael Patrick Welch & Alison Fensterstock, 978-1-60801-019-6 (2010)

Understanding the Music Business: A Comprehensive View edited by Harmon Greenblatt & Irwin Steinberg, 978-1-60801-004-2 (2010)

The Gravedigger by Rob Magnuson Smith, 978-1-60801-010-3 (2010)

Portraits: Photographs in New Orleans 1998-2009 by Jonathan Traviesa, 978-0-9706190-5-1 (2009)

**I hope it's not over, and good-by: Selected Poems of Everette Maddox* by Everette Maddox, 978-1-60801-000-4 (2009)

Theoretical Killings: Essays & Accidents by Steven Church, 978-0-9706190-6-8 (2009)

**Voices Rising: Stories from the Katrina Narrative Project* edited by Rebeca Antoine, 978-0-9728143-6-2 (2008)

On Higher Ground: The University of New Orleans at Fifty by Dr. Robert Dupont, 978-0-9728143-5-5 (2008)

The Change Cycle Handbook by Will Lannes, 978-0-9728143-9-3 (2008)

Us Four Plus Four: Eight Russian Poets Conversing translated by Don Mager, 978-0-9706190-4-4 (2008)

The El Cholo Feeling Passes by Fredrick Barton, 978-0-9728143-2-4 (2003)

A House Divided by Fredrick Barton, 978-0-9728143-1-7 (2003)

William Christenberry: Art & Family by J. Richard Gruber, 978-0-9706190-0-6 (2000)

The Neighborhood Story Project

New Orleans in 19 Movements by Thurgood Marshall Early College High School, 978-1-60801-069-1 (2011)

The Combination by Ashley Nelson, 978-1-60801-055-4 (2010)

Between Piety and Desire by Arlet Wylie and Sam Wylie, 978-1-60801-040-0 (2010)

The House of Dance and Feathers: A Museum by Ronald W. Lewis by Rachel Breunlin & Ronald W. Lewis, 978-0-9706190-7-5 (2009)

Beyond the Bricks by Daron Crawford & Pernell Russell, 978-1-60801-016-5 (2010)

Aunt Alice Vs. Bob Marley by Kareem Kennedy, 978-1-60801-013-4 (2010)

Signed, The President by Kenneth Phillips, 978-1-60801-015-8 (2010)

Houses of Beauty: From Englishtown to the Seventh Ward by Susan Henry, 978-1-60801-014-1 (2010)

Coming Out the Door for the Ninth Ward edited by Rachel Breunlin, 978-0-9706190-9-9 (2006)

Cornerstones: Celebrating the Everyday Monuments & Gathering Places of New Orleans edited by Rachel Breunlin, 978-0-9706190-3-7 (2008)

The Engaged Writers Series

Medea and Her War Machines by Ioan Flora, translated by Adam J. Sorkin, 978-1-60801-067-7 (2011)

Together by Julius Chingono and John Eppel, 978-1-60801-049-3 (2011)

Vegetal Sex (O Sexo Vegetal) by Sergio Medeiros, translated by Raymond L.Bianchi, 978-1-60801-046-2 (2010)

**Wounded Days (Los Días Heridos)* by Leticia Luna, translated by Toshiya Kamei, 978-1-60801-042-4 (2010)

When the Water Came: Evacuees of Hurricane Katrina by Cynthia Hogue & Rebecca Ross, 978-1-60801-012-7 (2010)

**A Passenger from the West* by Nabile Farès, translated by Peter Thompson, 978-1-60801-008-0 (2010)

**Everybody Knows What Time It Is* by Reginald Martin, 978-1-60801-011-0 (2010)

**Green Fields: Crime, Punishment, & a Boyhood Between* by Bob Cowser, Jr., 978-1-60801-018-9 (2010)

**Open Correspondence: An Epistolary Dialogue* by Abdelkébir Khatibi and Rita El Khayat, translated by Safoi Babana-Hampton, Valérie K. Orlando, Mary Vogl, 978-1-60801-021-9 (2010)

Gravestones (Lápidas) by Antonio Gamoneda, translated by Donald Wellman, 978-1-60801-002-8 (2009)

Hearing Your Story: Songs of History and Life for Sand Roses by Nabile Farès translated by Peter Thompson, 978-0-9728143-7-9 (2008)

The Katrina Papers: A Journal of Trauma and Recovery by Jerry W. Ward, Jr., 978-0-9728143-3-1 (2008)

Contemporary Poetry

Sheer Indefinite: Selected Poems, 1991-2012 by Skip Fox, 978-1-60801-080-6 (2011)

Atlanta Poets Group Anthology: The Lattice Inside by Atlanta Poets Group, 978-1-60801-064-6 (2011)

Makebelieve by Caitlin Scholl, 978-1-60801-056-1 (2011)

California Redemption Value by Kevin Opstedal, 978-1-60801-066-0 (2011)

Dear Oxygen: New and Selected Poems by Lewis MacAdams, edited by Kevin Opstedal, 978-1-60801-059-2 (2011)

Only More So by Tony Lopez, 978-1-60801-057-8 (2011)

Enridged by Brian Richards, 978-1-60801-047-9 (2011)

The Ezra Pound Center for Literature

Modernism and the Orient, edited by Zhaoming Qian, 978-1-60801-074-5 (2012)

A Gallery of Ghosts by John Gery, 978-0-9728143-4-8 (2008)

The Poets of the Sala Capizucchi (I Poeti della Sala Capizucchi) edited by Caterina Ricciardi and John Gery, 978-1-60801-068-4 (2011)

Trespassing, by Patrizia de Rachewiltz, 978-1-60801-060-8 (2011)

**The Imagist Poem: Modern Poetry in Miniature* edited by William Pratt, 978-0-9728143-8-6 (2008)